智者语录

——成功人生

吴 琼 苏焕宁◎译

青岛出版社
QINGDAO PUBLISHING HOUSE

图书在版编目（CIP）数据

智者语录．成功人生：英汉对照 / 吴琼，苏焕宁译．
—青岛：青岛出版社，2019.4
ISBN 978-7-5552-7053-9

Ⅰ．①智… Ⅱ．①吴… ②苏… Ⅲ．①英语—汉语—
对照读物②格言—汇编—世界 Ⅳ．①H319.4：H

中国版本图书馆 CIP 数据核字（2019）第 049356 号

书　　名　智者语录·成功人生（英汉对照）
译　　者　吴　琼　苏焕宁
出版发行　青岛出版社
社　　址　青岛市海尔路 182 号（266061）
本社网址　http://www.qdpub.com
邮购电话　0532-68068026
责任编辑　江伟霞　E-mail：wxjiang1206@163.com
封面设计　刘　晶
照　　排　青岛双星华信印刷有限公司
印　　刷　青岛国彩印刷有限公司
出版日期　2019 年 4 月第 1 版　2019 年 4 月第 1 次印刷
开　　本　32 开（787 mm × 1092 mm）
印　　张　8.25
字　　数　140 千
印　　数　1-6000
书　　号　ISBN 978-7-5552-7053-9
定　　价　32.00 元

编校印装质量、盗版监督服务电话　4006532017　0532-68068638

前 言

对于成功的诠释,众说纷纭,因人而异。军人以打胜仗为成功;商人以获得丰厚利润为成功;科学家以取得重要成果为成功。每个人都以完成自己的既定目标为成功。成功也就是完成非常想做的事情而获取的满足感。所以成功与目标紧密相关,如英国诗人叶芝所说,排除不可能达到的目标外,人生的满足感的程度取决于所选目标的高度。

要获取成功需要有适宜的外部的条件,更需具备相应的内在条件,如智慧、心态、性格、意志等。在外部条件差不多的情况下,目标方向、人的心态、学习能力、处事能力、意志力等因素便成了关键要素。有了目标,努力才会找到方向。要达到目标还需要坚定的信心,多一分信心,就多一分成功的把握。在前往成功彼岸的途中不会一帆风顺,这就需要在面对挫折和危机的时候,保持乐观和自信。要想获得成功,单打独斗是不行的,还需要一定的处事能力与合作精神,信任是合作的基石,互相协作,取长补短,学会倾听别人的观点,在合作中发展自己,合作才能共赢，合作加速成功。另外，成功还需要积极创新、勇于创新、打破常规、标新立异，创新思维比常规思维更容易带来成功。

要达到预定的目标，做事要专心致志，凡事要专注，专注就是用心，用心才会成功。要勇于进取，进取心是成功的要素，要有任劳任怨的敬业精神。要学会合理安排时间，要把时间集中用于对成功有益的事情上，为成功付出耐心，坚持不懈，成功属于善用时间的人。在获取成功的途中要不断学习，养成终身学习的习惯，善读无字之书，实践出真知，有计划地积累知识，在学习中不断调整自己的思路。有了目标，付诸行动更是成功的关键。有了目标不能束之高阁，而要用目标激励行动，在行动中实现目标，把计划变成现实，不要只生活在梦想里。

处事能力对成功的作用也不可小觑。要培养自己的责任感，责任感也是成功的动力。对小事负责才能担当大任。要培养坚强的自制力，控制自己让你更强大，不要成为情绪的奴隶，遇事冷静沉着，应付自如。要树立良好的信誉，人无信不立，勿以善小而不为，守护好自己善良的天性，要有感恩之心，感恩自己拥有的一切。

总而言之，人生的成功需要各种相关的外部条件和内在条件。这些条件便是获得成功的重要因素。为了更深入了解成功的诸要素,我们精选了相关的智者睿语,以供读者思考。所选内容也许会增加读者对成功的理解,也许有些具有画龙点睛的功效,让人读后豁然开朗,从此走上人生的成功之路,这也便是编译此书的初衷。

另外,本书也不失为学习英汉翻译的好助手,在领略智者的智慧之外,也许能从这些精心翻译的句子中悟出些翻译的诀窍,获得一些翻译乐趣,提高自己的翻译水平,有一些额外的收获。

徐莉娜老师对本书进行了修改和部分重译,在此一并致谢。

译　者

目　录

诠释成功

No one can cheat you out of ultimate success but yourselves.

除了自己,没有人能骗你们远离最后的成功。

Success too early often destroys a man easily.

成功太早,往往容易毁掉一个人。

Success is how high you bounce when you hit bottom.

成功取决于你在落到底时能反弹多高。

Don't confuse fame with success: Madonna is one; Helen Keller is the other.

不要将名气和成功混淆:麦当娜是前者,海伦·凯勒则是后者。

Success is never final and failure never fatal.

没有最终的成功,也没有致命的失败。

A man can find his place wherever he goes, so long as he is willing to pay for it .

只要一个人肯付出代价,他在哪里都能找到自己的天地。

Success is where the heart is.

心在哪里,成功就在哪里。

The more you love what you are doing, the more successful it will be for you.

——Jerry Gillies

越热爱所做的事情,事情就做得越成功。

——杰里·吉利斯

The trick is not how well you deal with success, but how well you deal with adversity.

成功的诀窍并不在于你是否善于应对成功,而在于你是否善于应对逆境。

Life consists not in holding good cards, but in playing well those you hold.

——J. Billings

生活不在于握有一手好牌,而在于把手里的牌打好。

——J·比林斯

Temporary achievements are gained in price of failure for years.

一时的成就是以多年的失败为代价取得的。

We can destroy ourselves by cynicism and disillusion, just as effectively as by bombs.

——Kenneth Clark

看破红尘、愤世嫉俗会像炸弹般摧毁我们。

——肯尼斯·克拉克

A tall tree catches the wind.

树大招风。

Easy come, easy go.

——Hazlitt

易得者亦易失。

——哈兹里特

There is only one success — to be able to spend your life in your own way.

——Christopher Morley

只有一种成功——能随心所欲过一生。

——克里斯托弗·莫利

The darkest hour is that before the dawn.

——Fuller

黎明前是最黑暗的时分。

——富勒

A great man is always willing to be little.

——R. W. Emerson

伟人总是愿意平易谦和。

——R・W・爱默生

As you sow you shall mow.

种瓜得瓜,种豆得豆。

It isn't by size that you win or fail —be the best of what you are.

成败不在大小,要让自己得到充分发挥。

A dignified failure is ten times better than an undignified success.

体面的失败比不体面的成功强十倍。

If you wish to succeed, you should use persistence as

your good friend, experience as your reference, prudence as your brother and hope as your sentry.

若要成功,当以恒心为良友,以经验为参谋,以谨慎为兄弟,并以希望为哨兵。

All will be accomplished for being respected and fail for being slighted.

百事之成,必在敬之; 凡有失败,必在轻慢。

Be not content with the minor success and one can become great mind. Be not lured by trivial benefits and one can make greater contributions.

不安于小成,方能成大器; 不惑于小利,方可建大功。

Success is the silver tint of the clouds of doubt.

成功是疑云中透出的一线银光。

When a big stone is in the way, the brave look on it as a stepping stone, the weak as an obstacle.

大石挡路,勇者将其看作垫脚石,弱者当成拦路虎。

Success covers a multitude of blunders.

成功包含大量的失误。

If you cherish your feather very much and avoid any injury, you will lose your two plumages, and they cannot fly in the sky any more.

珍爱自己的羽毛,使其不受一点损伤,便会失去两只翅膀,永不能凌空飞翔。

Ones who are over-confident will be in a weak and shaky position.

过分自信的人将会使自己处于脆弱而动摇的地位。

I'd rather lose in a cause that will one day win than win in a cause that will someday lose.

事业上与其赢得暂时的胜利,不如暂时失败而最终获胜。

Life is not a 100-meter dash, but more a cross-country run. If we sprint all the time, we not only fail to win the race, but never last long enough to reach the finish line.

生活不是百米冲刺,而更像越野长跑。一直疾跑,不仅赢不了比赛,而且根本坚持不到终点。

The most important single ingredient in the formula of success is to know how to get along with people.

善于和他人相处,是成功要素中最重要的。

One man has enthusiasm for 30 minutes, another for 30 days, but it is the man who has it for 30 years who makes a success of his life.

有的人热情只持续 30 分钟,有的人持续 30 天,而只有热情持续 30 年的人才能取得成功。

A good marksman may miss.

好射手也有失手的时候。

Success without honor is an unseasoned dish; it will satisfy your hunger, but it won’t taste good.

不光彩的成功就像没有调料的菜,可以消除饥饿,但味道不好。

You have to believe in yourself. That’s the secret of success.

必须相信自己,这是成功的秘诀。

The law of success should be relaxation but not tense.

成功的法则应该是放松，而不是紧张。

A failure is a man who has blundered, but is not able to cash in on the experience.

失败者就是犯了错误而不能从中吸取教训的人。

Success is the maximum utilization of the ability that you have.

成功就是最大限度地利用你所拥有的能力。

If you would hit the mark, you must aim a little above it. Every arrow that flies feels the attraction of earth.

要射靶心，瞄得须比靶心略高，离弦之箭都受地心引力的影响。

The man of great success neither be content with little favors nor be distressed by little adversity.

成大事者，不以小利而喜，不以小难而忧。

If we want to succeed in the world, we must be men of great wisdom but often appear slow witted.

要想成功，必须大智若愚。

Always bear in mind that your own resolution to succeed is more important than anything.

永远记住：成功的决心比什么都重要。

If A equals success, then the formula is A equals X plus Y plus Z, with X being work, Y play, and Z keeping your mouth shut.

——Albert Einstein

如果A等于成功，那公式就是：A=X+Y+Z，X是工作，Y是玩耍，Z是缄言。

——阿尔伯特·爱因斯坦

There are two ways of rising in the world, either by your own industry or by the folly of others.

成功之路有两条：靠自己的勤奋或靠他人的愚蠢。

To keep a lamp burning we have to keep putting oil in it.

想让灯一直亮，就必须不断给灯加油。

Often the best way to win is to forget to keep score.

获胜的最佳方法是忘记得分。

Victory won't come to me unless I go to it.

胜利不向我走来,我必须走向胜利。

A man can succeed at almost anything for which he has unlimited enthusiasm.

凡事倾注热情,几乎可以凡事必成。

To know how to wait is the great secret of success.

懂得如何等待,是成功的重要秘诀。

Fame usually comes to those who are thinking something else.

——O. W. Holmes

通常是没想到成名的人反而成了名。

——O · W · 霍姆斯

A life will be successful or not according as the power of accommodation is equal to or unequal to the strain of fusing and adjusting internal and external changes.

——Samuel Butler

人生的成功依赖于一个人的能力能否应对由适应内外变化而产生的压力。

——塞缪尔 · 巴特勒

Don't have to stay up nights to succeed; you have to stay awake days.

取得成功不必靠熬夜,而要靠白天保持清醒。

Don't regard yourself as giant when achieving success, and dwarf when having failure.

成功之时不要自视为巨人,失败之时不要自视为矮子。

When we are in the most difficult situation, we are not far from success.

最困难之时,也是离成功不远之日。

I never gave up, even when people told me I'd never made it.

我从不放弃,哪怕有人说我永远不会成功。

Be patient in adversity, be careful in favorable situation.

逆境中需要耐心,顺境中需要小心。

He who seizes the right moment, is the right man.

谁抓住时机,谁就是成功者。

A great vessel will be long in completion.

大器晚成。

You won't get ahead by trying to get even.

想跟别人看齐的人永远也走不到最前面。

Success is that old ABC — ability, breaks, and courage.

—— Charles Luckman

成功需要的就是老三样：能力、突破、勇气。

——查尔斯·卢克曼

Many a man owes his success to his first wife, and his second wife to his success.

许多男人将自己的成功归功于第一个妻子，而将第二个妻子归功于自己的成功。

It is not because things are difficult that we don't dare; it is because we don't dare that they are difficult.

并非事难而不敢为，而是不敢为而事难。

A dwarf on a giant's shoulders sees the farther of the two.

侏儒站在巨人的肩膀上，能比巨人看得远。

Those who dare to fail miserably can achieve greatly.

敢于破釜沉舟者方能成就伟业。

Success is to find the best in others.

成功就是发现别人的优点。

A confident person may turn the trivial into the great and the mean into the magic.

自信的人可以化渺小为伟大,化平庸为神奇。

Do not overrate what you have received, nor ever envy others. He who envies others does not obtain peace of mind.

不要高估所得,不要心存嫉妒。嫉妒者心不静。

It is a great matter to succeed in something under other's scorn because it proves you have not only conquered yourself but also your enemy.

被人藐视而成功,值得庆贺,证明你战胜了敌人,又战胜了自己。

The most secure way to avoid failure is the determination for success.

避免失败的最可靠方法就是下决心取得成功。

You may be disappointed if you fail, but you are doomed if you don't try.

失败会令人失望,但不尝试注定失败。

We see our past achievements as the end result of a clean forward thrust, and our present difficulties as signs of decline and decay.

我们会把已有的成就视为天花板,把眼前的困难视为衰败之兆。

Today's preparation determines tomorrow's achievement.

明天的成就取决于今天所做的准备。

A person who walks in another's tracks leaves no footprints.

沿袭他人的足迹难留自己的脚印。

If you want to succeed, you must make your own opportunities as you go.

你想成功,无论何处都须制造机会。

The success is nothing more than doing well whatever you do without a thought of fame.

——Henry Longfellow

成功无非是好好工作而不计功名。

——亨利·朗费罗

He conquers twice, who upon victory overcomes himself.

谁在夺取胜利之后又能征服自己,谁就赢得了两次胜利。

He has achieved success who has lived well, laughed often and loved much.

——Bessie A. Stanley

成功意味着生活富足,笑口常开,充满爱意。

——贝茜·A·斯坦利

It is sweat, not dew, that helps the harvest.

丰收不靠露滴,而靠汗水。

Winners fall, but they don't stay down. They stubbornly refuse to let a fall keep them from climbing.

成功者摔倒会爬起来,绝不会因摔倒而停止攀登。

Winners know they are not perfect. They respect their weaknesses while making the most of their strengths.

成功者有自知之明,正视弱点,充分发挥优点。

The strong always succeeds; the weakest goes to the wall.

坚强的人往往成功;软弱的人难免失败。

Early start makes easy stages.

先下手为强。

He that can have patience, can have what he will.

有耐心者事竟成。

He that returns good for evil obtains the victory.

胜利属于以德报怨的人。

Success is to win the respect of intelligent people and the affection of children.

成功就是赢得智者的尊敬和孩子的爱戴。

Winners take chances. They fear failing, but they refuse to let fear control them.

成功者敢于冒险，也害怕失败，但不会臣服于恐惧。

On earth there is no absolute success, but only constant striving.

世界上没有绝对成功，只有不断进取。

The people who get on in this world are the people who get up and look for circumstances they want, and if they cannot find them, make them.

——George Bernara Shaw

世上进取者会伺机而动，没有机会，便创造机会。

——乔治·萧伯纳

If you want to succeed you should strike out on new paths rather than travel the worn paths of accepted success.

若要成功，就要独辟蹊径，而非沿袭老路。

Towering genius disdains a beaten path. It seeks regions hitherto unexplored.

卓越的天才不屑走老路，而会另辟蹊径。

Energy and persistence conquer all things.

—— Benjamin Franklin

能量和毅力征服一切。

——本杰明·富兰克林

Hesitation is the mother of failure.

迟疑是失败之母。

A man who has an acute eyesight and a far-reaching understanding and acknowledges his limitation is not far from perfection.

目光敏锐,见解深刻,承认局限,便近乎完人。

We can't fly until we let go of the dirt.

丢下泥土,我们才能飞翔。

Winners don't blame fate for their failures; nor luck for their successes. Winners accept responsibility for their lives.

成功者不怨天尤人,也不相信运气,而是自负其责。

I would prefer even to fail with honor than win by cheating.

我宁愿虽败犹荣,也不愿欺骗取胜。

A watched pot is long in boiling.

心急水不沸。

If you consistently do your best, the worst will never happen.

——B. C. Forbes

你若坚持不懈,全力以赴,最坏的事情不会发生。

——B·C·福布斯

No, you never get any fun out of the things you haven't done.

没有春花焉得秋实?

Always aim at achievement and forget about success.

——Helen Hayes

争取做出成就,不计得失。

—— 海伦·荷斯

Good take-heed does surely speed.

小心谨慎加速成功。

You can't build a reputation on things you are going to do.

——Henry Ford

尚未成事，安得英名？

——亨利·福特

High achievers spot rich opportunities swiftly, make big decisions quickly, and move into action immediately. Follow these principles and you can make your dreams come true.

—— Robert Schuller

成就卓著者能捕捉良机，迅速决断，立刻行动。循此原则行事，梦想便能成真。

——罗伯特·舒勒

Success is the sum of small efforts, repeated day in and day out.

——Robert Collier

成功就是由夜以继日的一点点努力累积而成。

—— 罗伯特·科利尔

One never notices what has been done; one can only see what remains to be done.

——Marie Curie

切不要关注已做何事，只能看看何事要做。

——玛丽·居里

I might say that success is won by three things: first, effort; second, more effort; third, still more effort.

可以说赢得成功的三个前提是：努力，再努力，还要再努力。

All things are attained by diligence and toil.

一切都是通过勤劳获得的。

Let me tell you the secret that has led me to my goal. My strength lies solely in my tenacity.

——Louis Pasteur

告诉你我成功的秘密——我的优势只是坚持不懈。

——路易斯·巴斯德

When you get right down to the root of the meaning of the word "succeed", you find it simply means to follow through.

——F. W. Nichol

深究"成功"真实含义，不外乎紧追不舍。

——F·W·尼科尔

Luck is earned. Luck is working so hard at your craft, service or enterprise that sooner or later you get a break.

——Paul Hawken

幸运是争取来的。在从事的手艺、服务和事业上竭尽所能，迟早会时来运转。

——保罗·霍肯

If you do not think about the future, you cannot have one.

——John Gale

不为未来着想，就不会有未来。

——约翰·盖尔

Miracles sometimes occur, but one has to work terribly for them.

奇迹有时会发生，但你得为之拼命努力。

In order to succeed you must fail, so that you know what not to do next time.

——Anthony J. D'Angelo

为了成功，须先有失败，方能避免重蹈覆辙。

——安东尼·J·德安格罗

The talent of success is nothing more than doing well whatever you do without a thought of time.

成功之才不外乎凡事不计时间，精益求精。

If you're going to play the game properly you'd better know every rule.

——Barbara Jordan

要把游戏玩得好,就要知道游戏规则。

——巴巴拉·乔丹

A good name is easier lost than won.

名誉易失难得。

Remember what should be remembered, and forget what should be forgotten. Alter what is changeable, and accept what is not mutable.

记住该记住的,忘记该忘记的。改变能改变的,接受不能改变的。

Frequently looking at the bright and happy side is the secret of success all my life.

常向光明快乐的一面看,那就是我一生成功的秘诀。

The hardest thing about climbing the ladder of success is getting through the crowd at the bottom.

攀登成功阶梯最难的是要超越阶梯底部的拥挤人群。

Shortcuts to success often turn out to be trapdoors to failure.

成功的捷径常常是失败的陷阱。

Power invariably means both responsibility and danger .

权力总是意味着责任和危险。

The human being longs for a sense of being accomplished, of being able to do things with his hand, with his mind, with his will. Each of us wants to feel he or she has the ability to do something that is meaningful and that serves a tribute to our inherent abilities.

——Leonard R. Saylis

人们渴求成就感,渴望能够用自己的双手、头脑和意志办事。我们每个人都希望自己能够做出有意义并能显示出自己天赋的事来。

——里奥纳德 · R · 塞尔斯

A road of a thousand miles begins with one step.

千里之行始于足下。

Success is going from failure to failure without losing enthusiasm.

败而不馁,成功在望。

The landscape belongs to the man who looks at it.

——Ralph Waldo Emerson

风景属于赏景的人。

——拉尔夫·瓦尔多·爱默生

Many of life's failures are people who never realized how close they were to success until after they quit.

——Thomas Edison

许多生活中的失败者,往往在放弃了之后才意识到曾离成功是多么近。

——托马斯·爱迪生

He took a stumbling block and turned it into a stepping stone.

——Rev. Jesse Jackson

他把绊脚石变成了垫脚石。

——杰西·杰克森牧师

Self-distrust is the cause of most of our failures.

绝大多数的失败源于缺乏自信。

He that doth most at once doth least.

越想一次做最多,越是做得最少。/欲速则不达。

Your journey to success is a pathway that only you and you alone can take.

——Kurt Lee Hurley

成功之路只能由你,也只能由你自己去走。

——库尔特·李·赫尔利

Mishaps are like knives that either serve us or cut us as we grasp them by the handle or blade.

——James Russell Lowell

灾难就像刀子,握住刀柄可为己所用,握住刀刃则会割破手。

——詹姆斯·拉塞尔·洛威尔

A going foot it always getting.

腿勤生财。

Perseverance is the only road to success.

百折不挠是通向成功的唯一道路。

When one loves one's art, no service seems too hard.

——O. Henry

一旦热爱艺术,奉献并不难。

——欧·亨利

A man, like a watch, is to be valued by his manner of going.

——William Penn

人如手表,其价值取决于质量。

—— 威廉·潘恩

Diligence is the mother of good luck.

勤奋是幸运之母。

Diligence is the mother of success.

勤奋是成功之母。

To know how to wait is the great secret of success.

懂得如何等待是成功的重要秘诀。

I succeeded because I willed it; I never hesitated.

——Napoleon Bonaparte

我成功是因为我决意成功,从不踌躇。

——拿破仑·波拿巴

Achievement provides the only real pleasure in life.

——Thomas Edison

有所成就是人生唯一的真正乐趣。

——托马斯·爱迪生

If at first you don't succeed, try, try, try again.

初战未捷,那就努力再努力。

I have always observed that to succeed in the world one should seem like a fool, but be wise.

——Montesquieu

我总是发现,要成功于世,就必须大智若愚。

——孟德斯鸠

Success often depends upon knowing how long it will take to succeed.

成功常常取决于知道需要多长时间才能成功。

A will finds a way.

——Orison Swett Marden

有志者事竟成。

——奥里森·斯韦特·马登

We've learned from past experience that people just don't learn from past experience.

从经验得知经验总被忽视。

The difference between successful people and those that just don't get it is not whether you make mistakes or even provisionally fail, but how you respond to your failures and that you pick yourself up after each fall and continue on.

——Kurt Lee Hurley

成功人士与非成功人士的区别并不在于是否犯过错误,甚至是否暂时失败,而在于如何应对失败,在于每次跌倒之后如何振作起来,继续前行。

——库尔特·李·赫尔利

Success doesn't come quick; it doesn't come easy and should be painful enough to elicit deep introspection.

——Kurt Lee Hurley

成功不会转瞬即至,也不会轻易获得。成功之路充满痛苦,发人深省。

——库尔特·李·赫尔利

Don't watch the clock; do what it does. Don't stop.

——Sam Levenson

不要看表,而要像表一样不停地工作。

——萨姆·李文森

Life is a drama: it is not the length but the performance that matters.

人生如戏：重要的不是长度，而是表演水平。

There is no such thing as a great talent without great will-power.

——Balzac

没有伟大的意志力，便没有雄才伟略。

——巴尔扎克

There is no success without hardship.

没有艰辛便没有成功。

矢志不移

Nothing is impossible to a willing heart.

有志者事竟成。

Constant dropping wears the stone.

滴水穿石。

The secret of success is constancy of purpose.

矢志不移是成功的秘诀。

All that you do, do with your might; things done by halves are never done right.

——R. H. Stoddard

做一切事都应尽力为之,绝对不可半途而废。

——R·H·斯托达德

Diligence is near success.

勤奋近乎成功。

Some succeed because they are destined to; most succeed because they are determined to.

——Anatole France

有些人成功是命中注定,多数人成功源于坚定决心。

——阿纳托尔·法郎士

Act as if what you do makes a difference. It does.

——William James

像对待非凡之事一样而努力为之，结果便会真的不同凡响。

——威廉·詹姆斯

Slow and steady wins the race.

稳扎稳打，无往不胜。

The man who has made up his mind to win will never say "Impossible."

——Napoleon Bonaparte

决心取胜者从不说"不可能"。

——拿破仑·波拿巴

He who has never hoped can never despair.

——George Bernard Shaw

不抱希望的人绝不会失望。

——乔治·萧伯纳

To follow, without halt, one aim: there's the secret of success.

成功的秘密就是不停顿地向一个目标前进。

Confidence in yourself is the first step on the road to success.

自信是走向成功的第一步。

Never be unduly elated by victory or depressed by defeat.

——H. Porter

胜不矜,败不馁。

——H·波特

Try not to become a man of success but rather try to become a man of value.

——Albert Einstein

不要为成功而努力,要为做一个有价值的人而努力。

——阿尔伯特·爱因斯坦

Success belongs to the persevering.

成功属于不屈不挠的人。

Dare and the world always yields. If it beats you

sometimes, dare it again and again and it will succumb.

——W. M. Thackeray

大胆挑战,世界总会让步。有时败了,也要不断挑战,世界总会让步。

——W·M·萨克雷

Will, work and wait are the pyramidal cornerstones for success.

——Louis Pasteur

意志、工作和等待是成功金字塔的基石。

—— 路易斯·巴斯德

The important thing in life is to have a great aim, and the determination to attain it.

人生重要的是志存高远,矢志不移。

If you don't know what you're looking for in life, you will never find it.

如果生活没有目标,就会毫无所获。

He who has a "why" to live for can bear almost any "how".

——Nietzsche

有生活目标的人能忍受任何麻烦。

——尼采

Short of the impossible, as Yeats put it, the satisfaction we get from a lifetime depends on how high we choose our difficulties.

如叶芝所说,除了不可能达到的目标外,所选目标的难度决定人生的满足感。

God never tells us in advance whether the course we are to follow is the correct one.

上帝从来不会事先透露我们所走的方向是否正确。

All things come to those who go after them.

——B. J. Marshall

有志者事竟成。

——B·J·马歇尔

If a man wants his dream to come true, he must wake up.

要想实现梦想,须先从梦中醒来。

The lame man who keeps the right road outstrips the runner who takes a wrong one.

——Francis Bacon

瘸腿走对路也能超越跑错路的人。

——弗朗西斯·培根

A busy man is plagued with one desire, but a lazy one with a thousand.

忙人为一个目标而忙,懒人会为一千个欲望所困。

Discontent is the first step in progress.

不满足是前进的第一步。

Nothing in the world is difficult for one who sets his mind to it.

世上无难事,只怕有心人。

Nothing seek, nothing find.

没有追求就没有收获。

It is the dogged that does it.

有志者事竟成。

So long as you work hard enough, an iron rod can be ground into a needle.

只要功夫深，铁杵磨成针。

Where there is a will, there is a way.

有志者事竟成。

Great hopes make great man.

伟大抱负造就伟大人物。

The important thing in life is to have a great aim and the determination to attain it.

人生重要的事情在于确立一个伟大的目标，并决心使之实现。

Ideal is the beacon. Without ideal, there is no secure direction; without direction, there is no life.

理想是指路明灯。没有理想，就没有坚定的方向；没有方向，就没有生活。

Ideals are like the stars—we never reach them, but like mariners, we chart our course by them.

理想如星星，虽然够不到，但可以像水手那样靠星星把握航向。

The higher a person's ideal is, the purer his life is.

一个人的理想越崇高，生活就越纯洁。

Life without an aim is like sailing without the compass.

没有目标的生活，就像没有指南针的航行。

A genius is a person who aims at something no one else can see and hits it.

——Ervin Glapsy

天才追寻的目标别人看不到也达不到。

——欧文・格兰斯潘

There are things to aim at in life: first to get what you want and, after that, to enjoy it. Only the wisest of mankind can achieve the second.

生活目标是先获得想要的东西，之后享用。只有最明智的人才会享用。

You must have long-range goals to keep you from being frustrated by short-range failures.

有了长远目标,才不会因暂时的挫折而沮丧。

Never fear the space between your dreams and reality. If you can dream it, you can make it so.

不要担心梦想远离现实,有梦想就能实现。

Every life is a boat and the ideal is its sail.

每个人的生命都是一只小船,理想是它的风帆。

We are born with belief. A man with belief is like a tree growing apples.

我们生来就应该有信仰。一个有信仰的人,就像一棵会结苹果的树。

To reach definite destination, go along one way, but not wander on many roads.

要想到达既定的目的地,顺着一条路前进,不要在多条路上徘徊。

Men who have lost heart have never yet won a trophy.

失去信心的人永远得不到奖品。

We mustn't fear sunlight just because it almost always illuminates a miserable world.

不要因为阳光几乎总是照亮一个悲惨世界,我们就害怕阳光。

Reality is on one side. Ideal is on the other. Between flows torrential streams. Action is the bridge linking the two sides.

现实是此岸,理想是彼岸,中间隔着湍流,行动是架在河上的桥梁。

Life without ideals is no difference from death.

没有理想,等于死亡。

Hold fast to dreams, for if dreams die, life is a broken-winged bird that cannot fly.

Hold fast to dreams, for when dreams go, life is a barren field frozen with snow.

紧抓梦想,梦想一旦破灭,生活成了断翅小鸟,不能飞翔。

紧抓梦想,梦想一旦离去,生活就是冰封荒原,大雪茫茫。

Hope and courage are two bright diamonds in the crown of success.

希望和勇气是成功王冠上的两颗璀璨钻石。

An ideal will never give up a dogged pursuer. So long as you do not stop pursuing, you will bathe in the glow of your ideal.

理想从不抛弃执着的追求者,只要追求不止,你就会沐浴在理想的光辉之中。

The back of every creation, supporting it like an arch, is faith. But if one believes, miracles will occur.

信念如同拱架,是一切创造的支柱。人们有信念,奇迹就会出现。

People with goals succeed because they know where they are going.

有目标的人会取得成功,因为他们知道自己要去哪里。

In whatever position you find yourself determine first your objective.

无论处在何位,首先确定目标。

It's not where you came from that matters; it's where you're going.

来自何方不重要,去何方很重要。

Every road leads in two directions.

每条路都有两个方向。

The things a man has to have are hope and confidence in himself against odds.

希望与自信是逆境中必备的东西。

You can't cross the sea merely by standing and staring at the water. Don't let yourself indulge in vain wishes.

只是站着注视大海过不了海。不要沉溺于虚幻的希望之中。

Ideal is the sun of life.

理想是人生的太阳。

Hope and patience are two specific medicines to all, and the most reliable and comfortable things to those in adversity.

希望和耐心是所有人的特效药,是逆境中最抚慰人、最可靠的东西。

Hope is the second soul of the unlucky.

希望是不幸者的第二灵魂。

Self-confidence and self-reliance are the mainstays of a strong character.

自信和自立是坚强品格的支柱。

Self-confidence and hope are the privilege of youth.

自信和希望是青年的特权。

Don't believe that winning is really everything. It's more important to stand for something. If you don't stand for something, what do you win?

别以为取胜就是一切,更重要的是信念。如果没有信念,取胜又有何意义?

If your ambition is in the highest place, it is not a shame for you stay in the second or third highest place.

如果你志在最高处,那么即使待在第二或第三高处,也并不丢脸。

Ambition is the germ from which all growth of nobleness proceeds.

雄心是孕育一切高尚情操的种子。

A man without great aspirations is not worth the title of a great man even if he has some magnificent actions.

如果一个人胸无大志，即使再有壮举，也称不上是伟人。

Someone lives a life without any aim, just like a tiny grass in the river. They never walk but drift to the wind.

没有生活目标的人，就像河里的一叶小草，从不迈步，只是随波逐流。

To travel hopefully is better than to arrive.

充满希望的旅行比到达目的地更美妙。

We must accept finite disappointment, but we must never lose infinite hope.

我们必须接受有限的失望，但绝不可失去无限的希望。

Always keep your ideals high enough that you have to keep stretching to reach them.

理想要始终保持在你必须使劲伸手才能够得着的高度。

If you have a dream, give it a chance to happen.

如果有梦想,就给它实现的机会。

Hope is the best music for grief.

希望是悲痛中最佳音乐。

You can enjoy a grander sight, by climbing to a greater height.

欲穷千里目,更上一层楼。

Try to ascend the mountain's crest! It dwarfs all peaks under your feet.

会当凌绝顶,一览众山小。

Fear can keep us up all night long, but faith makes one fine pillow.

恐惧会使我们彻夜不眠,信念却是个好枕头。

Faith is the private capital which one saves in his home.

信念是储蓄在家里的私人资本。

Goals are dreams with deadlines.

目标就是带有最后期限的梦想。

If a man doesn't know what port he is steering for, no wind is favorable to him.

如果水手不知道要驶向哪个港口,那什么风都是不利的。

Goals serve as a stimulus to life.

目标是生命的兴奋剂。

Purpose is what gives life a meaning.

目标赋予生命以意义。

Hope is the source of life. Without hope, life will wilt.

希望是生命的源泉。失去希望,生命就会枯萎。

There is no winter on the earth of hope.

希望的土地上没有冬天。

An archer cannot hit the bulleye if he doesn't know where the target is.

如果弓箭手不知道靶子在哪里,就永远射不中靶心。

The world makes way for the man who knows where he is going.

知道前进的方向，世界会给他让路。

Putting your objective higher than your ability, your present life would be better than yesterday, and your future better than today.

让理想高于才干，你的今天才有可能超过昨天，你的明天才有可能超过今天。

The ideal of life is just to lead an ideal life.

生活的理想，就是理想地生活。

Look forward every day, and you'll have a new starting-point every day.

天天向前看，天天就有新起点。

If your ambition is on the summit, never stop halfway.

如果志在山顶，决不要半途而止。

Goals that are not written down are just wishes.

没有写下来的目标只是愿望而已。

A person can grow only as much as his horizon allows.

一个人的眼界有多宽，能力就会有多大。

No one can predict to what heights you can soar, even you will not know until you spread your wings.

谁都无法预言你能飞多高，如果不展开翅膀，你自己也无法知道。

Have an aim in life, or your energies will all be wasted.

——R. Peters

人生应该树立目标，否则你的精力会白白浪费。

——R·彼得斯

Only he who keeps his eyes fixed on the far horizon will find his right road.

只有高瞻远瞩，才能找准路线。

Choosing a goal and sticking to it changes everything.

选定目标并坚持到底就能改变一切。

Sight now what's near, while aiming at what's far.

放眼未来，着眼现在。

Love truth, but pardon error.

——Voltaire

热爱真理,但应宽恕错误。

——伏尔泰

An aim in life is the only fortune worth finding.

——Robert Louis Stevenson

生活目标是唯一值得寻找的财富。

——罗伯特·路易斯·史蒂文森

You can always find the sun within yourself if you will only search.

只要去寻找,你总能发现藏在你内心深处的太阳。

Even a small star shines in the darkness.

星星再小,在暗夜里也会发光。

Don't wait for what you want to come to you. Go after it with all that you are.

不要等待梦想实现,尽你所能去追它。

Purpose is the engine that fires your dream and your team.

目的是驱动梦想和团队的引擎。

He will shoot higher who shoots at the moon than he who aims at a tree.

瞄准月亮的人总比瞄准树木的人射得高。

Every time you stand up for an ideal, you send forth a tiny ripple of hope.

每当你捍卫理想时,希望的涟漪就会荡漾开来。

Not to self-praise for being content; not to quit for being defeated.

不可以一时得意,而自夸其能;也不可以一时失意,而自堕其志。

The higher you soar the more beautiful the view is.

飞得越高,看到的景色就越美。

No bird soars too high if he soars with his own wings.

鸟如果仅靠自己的翅膀飞翔,就飞不高。

Don't rush to achieve your goals; you may find yourself closer to where you want to be if you go more slowly.

不要急于求成,放慢速度将发现目标离自己更近。

The aim of life is to develop oneself and realize one's nature perfectly.

生活的目标就是不断发展自我,并完美实现自我。

You do not need to know how you're actually going to achieve a goal when you set it. Just repeatedly visualize the desired result, and the "how" will open up to you.

开始无须探究如何达到设定的目标。想要的结果不断展现,达到目标的办法就在眼前。

Whether or not you are able to achieve your goals in life, it is important to set them, and to strive for them.

设定目标,为之奋斗,至关重要,无论是否能否达到。

It is not enough to be industrious, so are the ants. what are you industrious for?

—— H. D. Thoreau

光勤劳不够,蚂蚁也勤劳。要看为什么而勤劳。

——H・D・梭罗

If you don't know what you're looking for in life, you will never find it.

如果生活没有目标,就会毫无所获。

Obstacles are those frightful things you see when you take your eyes off the goal.

——Hannah More

眼睛离开目标便会发现障碍很可怕。

——汉娜·摩尔

Do not , for one repulse, give up the purpose that you resolved to effect .

不要只因一次受挫就放弃决心想达到的目标。

He who has no idea about what to do the next day is the most misfortunate man.

不知道明天该做什么的人是最不幸的人。

We sail in the ocean of life by taking reason as compass, emotion as strong wind.

航行在生活的海洋里,要以理智为罗盘,以感情为大风。

The greatest achievement was at first and for a time a dream.

最伟大的成就最初一段时间只是梦想。

What's the gap between how you want to live and how you do live? Can you close it? Describe in detail your vision of the future for yourself — then work towards it.

期望的生活与目前的生活有何差距？能否消灭差距？详细构思未来的生活，然后为之奋斗。

You can never plan the future by the past.

——Burke

永远也不能依照过去来计划将来。

——伯克

Motivation is what gets you started. Habit is what keeps you going.

目标让你行动起来，习惯让你稳步前进。

Man can climb to the highest summit, but he cannot dwell there long.

——George Bernard Shaw

人可以爬到最高峰，但不能在那儿久住。

——乔治·萧伯纳

To travel is better than to arrive.

旅行胜于到达目的地。

Aim high, but don't let pursuing your goal become your only object in life.

人要心存高远,但不要把追逐目标当作唯一的生活目标。

Imagine yourself ten years from now. What would you like to happen? Set goals, and you may find you can realize them!

想象十年之内的自己,有何美好愿景? 设定目标,你会发现你能如愿以偿。

Life is a progress from want to want, not from enjoyment to enjoyment.

生活是从目标到目标的过程,而不是从享受到享受的过程。

That how many men there are in the world makes how many ways of life.

世界上有多少人,就有多少条生活道路。

The target of life is to grow.

人生的目标在于发展自己。

The great value of life is to spend it on something that will outlast it.

人生的伟大价值就是献身于比生命更持久的东西。

When you have too much to do, step back, and prioritize. That way, you can begin to work calmly towards your goal.

若太多事要做,退一步做规划,然后便可平静地向目标进发。

However much others expect of you, do not expect too much of yourself.

不管别人对你有多高的期望值,自己不要期望太高。

Success is achieved by converting each step into a goal and each goal into a step.

把每个步骤变成目标,再把每个目标变成步骤,便能成功。

What makes life dreary is the want of motive.

—— George Eliot

生活沉闷,因为缺乏动力。

——乔治 · 艾略特

It's so hard when I have to, and so easy when I want to.

事情在不得不做时很难,想做时很容易。

A great career needs unswerving spirit.

伟大的事业需要始终不渝的精神。

Only perseverance, is the key to success.

唯坚忍二字,为成功之要诀。

Although patience and persistence is a painful thing, but it can gradually bring you good.

忍耐和坚持虽是痛苦的事情,但却能渐渐地为你带来好处。

学无止境

Genius without education is like silver in the mine.

未受教育的天才犹如矿中之银。

A teacher affects eternity; he can never tell where his influence stops.

——H. B. Adams

教师的影响是永恒的；他无法估计自己的影响会有多深远。

——H·B·亚当斯

If you want to jump high over an obstacle, you must take a long run up to it first.

逾越障碍,需先助跑。

Knowledge is a city to the building of which every human being brought a stone.

——Emerson

知识是一座城市,每个人都为其建筑增砖添瓦。

——爱默生

Real knowledge, like everything else of value, is not to be obtained easily, it must be worked for, studied for, thought for, and more than all, must be prayed for.

——Thomas Arnold

真知如宝物，不会唾手可得，非经挖掘、研究、思考，特别是渴求，难以获得。

——托马斯·阿诺德

A person is not an empty bottle that can be filled with any liquid.

人不是可以注入任何液体的空瓶子。

If you doubt yourself , then indeed you stand on shaky ground.

怀疑自己，立足点不稳。

Knowledge comes from experience alone.

知识的唯一来源便是实践。

Knowledge makes humble, ignorance makes proud.

知识使人谦虚，无知使人骄傲。

Knowledge is power.

——Francis Bacon

知识就是力量。

——弗朗西斯·培根

Knowledge is a treasure, but practice is the key to it.

知识是宝库,实践是宝库的钥匙。

Knowledge is the food of the soul.

——Plato

知识是心灵的食粮。

——柏拉图

Knowledge is the great sun in the firmament. Life and power are scattered with all its beams.

——Daniel Webster

知识如空中太阳,其光芒散播生命和力量。

——丹尼尔·韦伯斯特

Learning is the eye of the mind.

学习让心灵开窍。

What is learned in the cradle is carried to the grave.

幼年所学,终生不忘。

Learn from the mistakes of others and prevent your own.

前车之鉴,后事之师。

Learn to creep before you leap.

先学爬,后学跳。

Without learning, without eyes.

没有知识,如同盲人。

He who will not learn when he is young will regret it when he is old.

少壮不努力,老大徒伤悲。

It's a fine thing to have ability, but the ability to discover ability in others is the true test.

——Elbert Hubbard

有才固然好,识才是真才。

——阿尔伯特·哈伯德

Learning is a bitter root, but it bears sweet fruit.

学习根苦果甜。

Learning is like rowing upstream; not to advance is to drop back.

学习如逆水行舟，不进则退。

If you don't learn to think when you are young , you may never learn .

年轻时没有学会思考，就永远学不会思考。

Education should not merely have intelligence in mind and it must try to make the educated sharper, more civilized and more benevolent.

教育不该只从智力上着眼，必须力求使受教育者更机敏、更文明、更仁爱。

The proper force of words lies not in the words themselves, but in their application.

语言的威力不在于词语本身，而在于它们的使用。

A knowledgeable person is like true gold, and will be respected wherever he goes.

有学问的人像真金，无论走到什么地方都会受人尊敬。

Knowledge is like dynamite—dangerous unless handled wisely.

知识如同炸药——处理不当是很危险的。

For a modest man, achievements serve as a vaulting-pole; for a conceited man, achievements serve as a slide.

成绩是谦虚者的撑竿,是骄傲者的滑梯。

Any one who conducts an argument by appealing to authority is not using his intelligence, he is just using his memory.

引经据典辩论,不是用才智,只是靠记忆而已。

Knowledge is like a wild horse. He will belong to a person who can rein him.

知识像野马,谁能驾驭它,它就属于谁。

Knowledge may give weight, but accomplishments give luster, and many more people see luster than weight.

知识给人以分量,而成就给人以光泽,更多的人看重光泽而非分量。

Whatever things in the world can be easily satisfied except two things: one is reading, and the other is love.

世上无论何事,都很容易满足,唯有两件事不能:一是读书,一是爱情。

Knowledge is the candle to conduct you to the bright and true life.

知识如烛光,引人走向光明的真正人生。

In science, read, by preference, the newest books; in literature, the oldest.

科学著作,最好读最新的书;文学著作,最好看最经典的书。

Book is a good company that has encyclopedic mind, but it never talks wordily. When you long for it, it teaches you elaborately, but it never nags you endlessly.

书是好伙伴,满腹经纶,却不喋喋不休。你非常需要时,它悉心指教,却从不无休止地纠缠。

A room without books is a body without soul.

没有书的房间就像没有灵魂的躯体。

Great nations write their autobiographies in three manuscripts—the book of their deeds, the book of their words and the book of their art.

伟大的民族用三种方式写自传——行为之书、言语之书和艺术之书。

Ideal books are the key to one's wit.

理想的书是智慧的钥匙。

Knowledge is power, but enthusiasm pulls the switch.

知识就是电源，但热情是开关。

A great book should leave you with many experiences.

一本好书应该给你增加许多经验。

Education is a progressive discovery of our ignorance.

教育能使人逐渐发现自己的无知。

Education makes a people easy to lead, but difficult to drive; easy to govern but impossible to slave.

教育使一个民族容易领导，但难以驱使；容易治理，但无法奴役。

Knowledge is the garland on the head.

知识是头上的花环。

The simplest question is also the most difficult one.

最简单的问题,也是最难回答的问题。

Not knowing one's own ignorance is doubly ignorant.

不知道自己的无知,乃是双倍的无知。

Knowledge is like a fishnet; the wider and stronger it is, the more fish it catches.

知识像渔网,网越宽越牢,网住的鱼就越多。

An experienced man reads with two eyes, one seeing the literal words, the other seeing through the back.

经验丰富的人读书用两只眼睛,一只眼睛看到纸面上的话,另一只眼睛看到言外之意。

Learning without thought is useless; thought without learning is perilous.

学而不思则罔,思而不学则殆。

Learning is sunshine. Ignorance is darkness.

学问是阳光，无知是黑暗。

Nurture is above nature.

教养重于天赋。

Knowledge is like the spring underground—the deeper you dig, the clearer the water is.

知识好像地下的泉水，掘得越深，水就越清。

Books are for use, not for show; you should own no book that you are afraid to mark up, or afraid to place on the table, wide open and face down.

书是用的，不是摆设；怕在上面做记号或怕摊开反扣在桌子上的书，不应拥有。

What education is to the heart is what sculpture is to the marble.

教育之于心灵，犹如雕刻之于大理石。

It is a good book opened with expectation and closed with profit.

好书开卷引人入胜，闭卷使人受益。

Read not to contradict and confute, not to believe and take for granted, nor to find talk and discourse, but to weigh and consider.

读书时不可存心诘难作者,不可尽信书中之言,也不可断章取义,而应推敲细思。

A good book often serves as a match to light the dormant powder within us.

一本好书经常起着一根火柴的作用——点燃我们心中潜在的火药。

A good book is the purest essence of a human soul.

一本好书是一个人灵魂最纯净的结晶。

Reading is like eating. If you chew it unhurriedly, the taste will keep for long. If you chew it hurriedly, you won't know the taste.

读书犹如饮食,从容咀嚼,回味无穷;狼吞虎咽,不知其味。

Reading in youth is like peeping the moon through a crack; at middle age, like looking over it in a courtyard; at old age, like playing it on a platform.

少年读书,如隙中窥月;中年读书,像庭中望月;老年读书,似台上赏月。

The beautiful thing about learning is nobody can take it away from you.

学识的妙处在于,谁也无法将它从你那里夺走。

Though one may have read many volumes of books, learning without inquiring will make him only a stupid man.

读书万卷,学而不问,可称憨。

Digesting a page of book carefully is better than reading a book hurriedly.

把一页书好好消化,胜过匆匆阅读一本书。

Zeal without knowledge is frenzy.

没有知识的热情是狂热。

Books are the ship crossing the sea of time.

书籍是横渡时间之海的航船。

It is better to place the books in the study than to stuff the money into your pocket.

书房里摆满书籍远比钱包里塞满钞票要好。

All those who offered me a piece of good advice are my teachers.

赐吾建言者,皆吾师也。

It is a kind of perfect enjoyment to like reading; other kinds of enjoyment may come to an end, but reading books lends people permanent enjoyment.

爱读书是一种完美的享受。别的享受都有尽头,而读书给人的享受却永无止境 。

To know that we know what we know, and that we don’t know what we don’t know, this is true knowledge.

知之为知之,不知为不知,乃真知也。

Books can either make us traveling all over the world or have a heart to heart talk with us though strange to us.

书能使我们足不出户而畅游世界,素不相识而促膝谈心。

A bad book is like a bad friend, who may kill you.

坏书就像损友,会把你戕害。

Knowledge makes a man elegant, but communications make him perfect.

知识使人文雅,交流使人完善。

Man cannot be without teachers.

人不可无师。

Books are the advisor in hand anytime.

书是随时随身顾问。

It is harder to conceal ignorance than to acquire knowledge.

掩盖无知要比学到知识更难。

Books are not made for furniture, but there is nothing else that so beautifully furnishes a house.

图书不是用来装饰房间的,但任何东西也没有它装饰的房间美丽。

Knowledge is the best honor of the young, the biggest consolation of the old, the most precious treasure of the poor and the most expensive ornament of the rich.

知识是年轻人的最佳荣誉、老年人的最大慰藉、穷人的最宝贵财富和富人的最贵饰品。

In learning something, one should respect his teacher the most.

为学要先尊师。

No teacher in your life, no gain in your wit.

人生不从师,心智难开启。

Human life is limited, but knowledge is limitless.

人生有涯,知无涯。

In expanding the field of knowledge, we but increase the horizon of ignorance.

扩大知识面时,也在扩大无知面。

Excellent books are like a wise and good elder, support me moving forward step by step, and gradually know the world.

好书像聪明的善良长者,扶我一步步前行,让我一步步了解世界。

Verbalism is the shadow of action.

言辞是行动的影子。

Words are like leaves; and where they most abound, much fruit of sense beneath is rarely found.

言辞犹如树叶；树叶最茂密的地方很难找到丰硕的理智之果。

When doing some learning, one should, like piloting a submarine, be able to dive deep into the ocean of knowledge and rise to the surface as well.

做学问要像驾驶潜水艇那样,既能钻进知识海洋的深处,又能浮出水面。

Knowledge rests not upon truth alone, but upon error also.

知识不仅有赖于真理,也有赖于谬误。

A man without knowledge is like a house without a foundation.

人没有知识,就像房子没有地基。

There is a big difference between an eager person who wants to read a book and a tired person who wants a book to read.

渴望看书的人与因无聊而看书的人有天壤之别。

To be ignorant of one's ignorance is the malady of the ignorant.

不知道自己的无知是无知者的可悲之处。

The more you know, the less you would like to waste your time.

知识越多,越不喜欢浪费时间。

A truly great book should be read in youth, again in maturity and once more in old age, as a fine building should be seen by morning light, at noon and by moonlight.

——Robertson Davies

一部真正的杰作应该在年轻时读,成年后再读,最后在老年时还要读。正如一个优美的建筑应该在晨光中看,中午再看,最后还要在月光中看。

——罗伯特逊·戴维斯

People with tact have less to retract.

——Arnold Glasgow

智者悔少。

—— 阿诺德·格拉斯哥

Wisdom in the mind is better than money in the hand.

脑中智慧胜于手中金钱。

Books are a flight of stairs for the human progress.

书籍是人类进步的阶梯。

The highest intellects, like the tops of mountains, are the first to catch and to reflect the dawn.

才智最高的人就像山峰那样,最早发现并反射曙光。

All book are written for helping your idea but not for replacing your idea.

一切书都是为助你思考,而非替你思考而写的。

A book is life with visible characters. Men of passion can deeply understand it.

书是有字的生活,感情丰富的人才能深刻领会。

One’s sole enemy is ignorance.

人唯一的敌人就是无知。

Nothing is stronger than knowledge, so man with knowledge is invincible.

任何力量都没有知识强大,用知识武装起来的人是不可战胜的。

Books and friends should be few but good.

书和朋友不在多而在好。

Plants of learning must be watered with the rain of tears.

知识的幼苗要用泪雨来浇灌。

Example is always more efficacious than precept.

——Samuel Johnson

身教胜于言教。

——塞缪尔·约翰逊

Mistakes are an essential part of education.

——Bertrand Russell

从错误中吸取教训是教育极为重要的一部分。

——伯特兰·罗素

Every person has two educations, one which he receives from others, and one, more important, which he gives to himself.

——Edward Gibbon

每个人都受两种教育，一种来自别人，另一种更重要的是来自自己。

——爱德华·吉朋

Education is the transmission of civilization.

——Will Drant

教育传播文明。

——维尔·杜兰特

Education is not the filling of a pail but the lighting of a fire.

——William Butler Yeats

教育不是注满一桶水，而且点燃一把火。

——威廉·巴特勒·叶芝

Better be unborn than untaught, for ignorance is the root of misfortune.

——Plato

不受教育，不如不出世，因为无知是不幸的根源。

——柏拉图

Education commences at the mother's knee, and every

word spoken within the hearsay of children tends towards the formation of character.

——Hosea Ballou

教育始于母亲膝下,孩童性格在耳濡目染中形成。

——何西阿 · 巴卢

Education does not mean teaching people to know what they do not know; it means teaching them to behave as they do not behave.

——John Ruskin

教育的意义不在于传授知识,而在于改变人的行为方式。

——约翰 · 罗斯金

Education is a progressive discovery of our ignorance.

——Will Durant

教育是一个逐步发现自己无知的过程。

——维尔 · 杜兰特

Education has for its object the formation of character.

——Herbert Spencer

教育是以造就人的品质为其目标的。

——赫伯特·斯宾塞

Education has produced a vast population able to read but unable to distinguish what is worth reading.

——George Macaulay Trevelyan

教育造就了一大批能读书却不会识别什么书值得读的人。

——乔治·麦考利·特里维廉

Life itself, without the assistance of colleges and universities, is becoming an advanced institution of learning.

即使没有学院和大学教育,人生本身也会成为一所高等学府。

Education is the chief defence of nations.

——Edmund Bruke

教育是国家的主要防御力量。

——埃德蒙·伯克

Cleanliness and order are not matters of instinct; they

are matters of education, and like most great things, you must cultivate a taste for them.

——Benjamin Disraeli

整洁并非出自本能,而是学来的。像对大多数重要的喜好一样,对整洁的喜好也必须培养。

——本杰明·迪斯雷利

For a cultivated man to be ignorant of foreign languages is a great inconvenience.

——Anton P. Chekhov

受过教育的人不懂外语是极不方便的。

——安东·P·契克夫

I have long since abandoned the notion that higher education is essential to either success or happiness. Hot houses of learning do not always grow anything edible.

——Robert Moses

我早就不认为高等教育是通往成功或幸福之路。知识温室培育出的并非总是可用之才。

——罗伯特·摩西

Let early education be a sort of amusement; you will then be better able to find out the natural bent.

——Plato

初期教育应是一种娱乐,这样才更能发现一个人的自然爱好。

——柏拉图

The great difficulty in education is to get experience out of ideas.

——G. Santayana

教育的难处在于理论指导实践。

——G·桑塔亚那

Life surrounds us with teachers, if we are but willing to learn. Actually, everyone and everything in our life are our teachers — they teach by example of something we'd like to attain or something we'd like to abandon.

——Marie T. Russell

愿学习者,生活处处皆老师。事实上,人人可为师,事事可为师——择其善者而从之,其不善者而改之。

——玛丽·T·罗素

付诸行动

Take time to deliberate, but when the time for action arrives, stop thinking and go in.

——John Albion Andrew

要深思熟虑,一旦可以行动,就要毫不犹豫,马上行动。

——约翰·阿尔比·安德鲁

Affairs that are done by due degrees are soon ended.

事情要按部就班地做,很快就会做完。

A good beginning is half done.

良好的开端是成功的一半。

Plant your own garden and decorate you own soul, instead of waiting for someone to bring you flowers.

种好自己的花园,装饰自己的心灵,而不是坐等别人带给你鲜花。

Industry is the soul of business and the keystone of prosperity.

勤劳是事业的灵魂,是成功的基石。

Character cannot be developed in ease and quiet. Only through experience of trial and suffering can the soul be strengthened, ambition inspired, and success achieved.

——Helen Keller

性格不能在平和安逸的环境中得到锻炼。考验与磨难能够锤炼心灵，激励志向，带来成功。

——海伦·凯勒

Sow a Thought, Reap an Act, Sow an Act, Reap a Habit, Sow a Habit, Reap a Character, Sow a Character, Reap a Destiny.

—— Ralph Waldo Emerson

种下思想，收获行动；种下行动，收获习惯；种下习惯，收获性格；种下性格，收获命运。

——拉尔夫·瓦尔多·爱默生

Custom is a second nature.

习惯是第二天性。

It is while you are patiently toiling at the little tasks of life that the meaning and shape of great whole of life dawn on you.

——P. Brooks

只有在耐心操持生活琐事时，你才能领悟整个生活的意义，了解生活的真面目。

——P·布鲁克斯

A professional is someone who can do his best work when he doesn't feel like it.

——Alistair Cooke

专业人士做事情时，不愿意做也要做到最好。

——阿利斯泰尔·库克

Habit is a cable. We weave a thread of it each day, and at last we cannot break it.

习惯是缆绳，每天编入一股，最终便积习难改。

Whatever you do, do it with love. Then it will be well done.

做一事，爱一事，事事成功。

Don't do nothing because you can't do everything. Do something. Do anything.

—— Colleen Patrick-Goudreau

不要因为不能无所不做就什么也不做。做些事，做任何事。

——科林·帕特里克·古德罗

It's so hard when I have to, and so easy when I want to.

事情在不得不做时很难，想做时很容易。

Watch your thoughts; they become words. Watch your words; they become actions. Watch your actions; they become habits. Watch your habits; they become character. Watch your character; it becomes your destiny.

——Ray Bradbury

思维要严谨，它将成为言谈；言谈要慎重，它将成为行动；行动要谨慎，它将成为习惯；习惯要关注，它将成为性格；性格要塑造，它将成为命运。

——雷·布拉德伯里

Choose always the way that seems the best, however rough it may be; custom will soon render it easy and agreeable.

再难也要择良方而为之，反复练习，习惯后很快便会得心应手。

Judge each day not by the harvest you reap but by the seeds you plant.

—— Robert Louis Stevenson

要看每日成绩大小，不看收获大小，要看播种多少。

——罗伯特·路易斯·史蒂文森

Optimism, unaccompanied by personal effort, is merely a state of mind and not fruitful.

乐观而没有付出，也只是乐观而一无所获。

To those who waste life, their youth will fade, and life will desert them.

谁虚度年华，青春就要褪色，生活就会抛弃他们。

Custom makes all things easy.

有个好习惯，事事皆不难。

The question for each man to settle is not what he would do if he had means, time, influence, and educational advantages, but what he will do with the things he has.

——Hamilton Wright Mabie

每人都要解决的问题并非等有办法、时间、影响、教育优势后该做什么，而是当前条件下该做什么。

——汉密尔顿·莱特·梅彼

Our main business is not to see what lies dimly at a distance, but to do what lies clearly at hand.

我们的主要任务不是盯着远处模糊不清的东西，而是要着手处理摆在眼前的事情。

Custom reconciles us to everything.

习惯成自然。

The second half of a man's life is made up of nothing but the habits he has acquired during the first half.

——Fyodor Dostoevsky

人的后半生只不过是由其前半生形成的习惯而构成。

——陀思妥耶夫斯基

Better do more daily, trivial, ordinary and practical work that is needed by the people, than say a thousand empty words that may be sweet to the ear.

多做一些人们需要的、日常细小的、平凡而又实际的工作,胜过说一千句漂亮动听的话。

We cannot change anything unless we accept it. Condemnation does not liberate it, it oppresses.

——Carl Jung

对任何事情我们必先接受它,才能改变它。指责抱怨无济于事,我们别无选择。

——卡尔·荣格

Activity in the back of a very small idea will produce more than inactivity and the planning of a genius.

—— James A. Worsham

很小主意变为行动胜于束之高阁的天才计划。

——詹姆斯·A·沃瑟姆

A thought which does not result in an action is nothing much, and an action which does not proceed from a thought is nothing at all.

——Georges Bernanos

思想不带来行动则意义不大,而行动不源于思想则毫无意义。

——乔治·贝那诺斯

You can only do your best in life, and no more.

人生只能尽力而为。

A man without worry is like a dog without the master.

人没有了操心的事,就像狗没有了主人。

Even if you're on the right track, you'll get run over if you just sit there.

即使你在正确的跑道上，如果只是坐在那里，也会被超越。

A generation without a cause in its youth has no legacy in its old age.

年轻时没有事业，年老时就不会留下遗产。

The people deep in the spring scenery and oblivious of industrious work cannot have the autumn harvest.

沉醉于春光而忘却辛勤劳动，就不能获得秋后的硕果。

The only way to live is to accept each minute as an unrepeatable miracle.

生活的唯一方法就是把每一分钟都当作无法重复的奇迹。

The society won't treat someone with generosity unless he proves himself to the society that he is worthy of being treated in this way.

社会不会厚待一个人，除非他自己向社会证明他值得厚待。

We soon believe what we desire.

——Chaucer

只要是所渴求的，我们很快就信以为真。

——乔叟

The people who succeed in life are those who know that they are not clever but work hard to make up for their inefficiency.

生活中成功的人是那些自知不聪明而努力工作以弥补不足的人。

Life has never been simple and easy; even if you live in pleasure and amenity, you may still run into difficulties you need to overcome.

生活从不简单容易，即使你生活得快乐如意，也会遇到需要克服的困难。

One must seek pillar in life! Without it, life is boring even if no problem.

人必须在生活中寻求支柱！如果没有这个支柱，即使没有问题，生活也会乏味。

Never place our hopes on allies in the life battle.

在人生战场上，决不要寄希望于盟军的支持。

Do not dwell in the past, do not dream of the future; concentrate the mind on the present moment.

不要沉湎于过去或幻想于未来，要关注今天。

A man, if not gone through sorrows and joys, not fight hand to hand with life, cannot understand the real meaning of life.

如果不经历悲欢离合，不和生活赤手搏斗，就不可能懂得人生的真正意义。

One's life may kindle or decay. I shouldn't decay. I would kindle!

人的一生可能燃烧，也可能腐朽。我不应腐朽。我要燃烧！

It will never rain roses. When we want to have more roses, we must plant trees.

——George Eliot

天上绝不会不会掉玫瑰，想要更多玫瑰，必须自己栽培。

——乔治·艾略特

Perhaps you can't control your job, but you may be able to make other changes in your life.

——Alan L. Mcginnis

或许你不能支配自己的工作,但你却能让生活有所变化。

——艾伦·L·麦金尼斯

That how many men there are in the world makes how many ways of life.

世界上有多少人,就有多少条生活道路。

Life is like the rugby race whose rule is to strive for the bottom-line.

生活好比橄榄球比赛,其规则就是奋力冲向底线。

All that is noble is in itself of a quiet nature, and appears to sleep until it is aroused and summoned forth by contrast.

——Goethe

一切崇高的事物自然恬静,仿佛沉睡,只有在对比中其崇高的品质才得以唤醒,得以彰显。

——歌德

The art of living is more like wrestling than dancing.

生活的艺术像摔跤,而不像跳舞。

Passion is like the wind that fills the sails of a ship; if it blows too hard, the ship will sink; but if it doesn't blow at all, the ship cannot sail on.

激情如同吹动帆船的风,太大会把船吹沉;不吹,船就不动。

I'd rather regret the things I've done than the things I haven't.

——Lucille Ball

宁愿为做过的事情后悔,也不愿意为没有做的事情后悔。

——露西尔·鲍尔

Each small task of everyday life is part of the total harmony of the universe.

日常生活中每做一事都是和谐世界的一部分。

If a job is worth doing, it's worth doing well.

值得做的工作就值得做好。

Life is raw material. We are artisans. We can sculpt our existence into something beautiful, or debase it into ugliness. It's in our hands.

生命是原材料,我们是匠人,生命的美与丑全取决于自己。

Remember, when life's path is steep, keep your mind even.

记住,生活道路陡峭时,心要保持平稳。

Life is a leaf of white paper, thereon each of us may write his word or two.

人生就像一张白纸,每个人都可以在上面写上一两个字。

Our very business in life is not to get ahead of others, but to get ahead of ourselves.

人生要做的不是赶超别人,而是突破自我。

The path of life is overgrown with brambles, but a successful person can brighten his journey up with the light of hope, and burn the brambles away with the fire of patience.

人生道路上布满荆棘,但成功者能用希望之光照亮旅途,用坚忍之火烧尽那些荆棘。

In life as in a football game, the principle to follow is: hit the line hard.

人生就像一场足球赛,遵循的原则是:努力射门。

Great things are done by a series of small things brought together.

——Vincent van Gogh

万里之行始于足下,不积跬步无以至千里。

——文森特·梵高

To exist is to change, to change is to mature, to mature is to go on creating oneself endlessly.

——Henri Bergson

存在即变化,变化即成熟,成熟即不断地改革自新。

——亨利·勃格森

Actions speak louder than words.

干比说更有说服力。

Saying and doing are two different things.

说是一回事,做事另一回事。

From small beginnings comes great things.

万里之行,始于足下。

The three great essentials to achieve anything worthwhile are, first, hard work; second, stick-to-itiveness; third, common sense.

——Thomas Edison

获得任何成就需要三个最基本的重要条件：第一,苦干；第二,毅力；第三,常识。

——托马斯·爱迪生

Life doesn't believe tears but only cheers those who press forward in the face of difficulties.

生活不相信眼泪,它只为那些知难而进的人喝彩。

What's a man's first duty? The answer's brief: to be himself.

——Ibsen

人的第一职责是什么？答案很简单：做自己。

——易卜生

Great works are performed not by strength but by perseverance.

恒心而非力量成就伟业。

The best way to predict your future is to create it

预测未来的最好办法就是创造未来。

Experience is the best, and sternest teacher.

经验是最好、最严厉的老师。

Life is like a dog-sled team. If you aren't in the lead, the scenery never will change.

人生像狗拉雪橇队。如果你不是领头犬,风景永远不会改变。

Variety is the spice of life.

变化是生活的调味品。

Life is measured by thought and action, not by time.

——J. Lubbock

衡量生命的尺度是思想和行动,而不是时间。

——J·卢伯克

The secret to a rich life is to have more beginnings than endings.

生活丰富多彩的秘诀，就是开始的多，结束的少。

The innovator is not an opponent of the old, he is a proponent of the new.

——Lyle E. Shaller

改革者就是革旧图新的人。

——莱尔·E·夏勒

Discovery is seeing what everybody else has seen, and thinking what nobody else has thought.

发现就是看见其他人所熟视无睹，思考其他人所未曾思考。

If one wants to use a fleeting opportunity, one has to be prepared both in finance and mind.

如果想利用稍纵即逝的机会，一个人就得做好物资上和精神上的双重准备。

When written in Chinese, the word "crisis" is composed of two characters—one represents danger, and the other represents opportunity.

在汉语里，“危机”是由两个字组成的——一个代表危险，一个代表机会。

Chances appear before everyone, but the question is whether to grasp it or not. This is the crossroad of life.

人人面前都会出现机会，问题在于你能否抓住它。机会是人生的十字路口。

Opportunity's favorite disguise is trouble.

机会最爱的伪装就是麻烦。

It's hard to tell whether the opportunity or the trap is more, because the opportunity is often the trap, but the possibility of discovering the opportunity is not excluded from the trap.

很难说生活中是机会多还是陷阱多，因为机会常常就是陷阱，而陷阱里也不排除发现机会的可能。

Opportunities are never lost; someone will take the ones you miss.

机遇决不会消失，有人会抓住你错过的机会。

把握人生

The trouble of life consists in choosing.

人生的难处在于选择。

Life is essentially an art of broad sense.

人生本来就是一种广义的艺术。

A different language is a different vision of life.

不同的语言有不同的人生注解。

The good or ill of man lies within his own will.

——Epictetus

人善良或邪恶在他自己的意志之中。

——埃比克泰德

He is born in a good hour who gets a good name.

生逢其时，美誉自至。

Youth is the most charming when it will vanish.

青春在它即将逝去时最具魅力。

Every flow has its ebb.

潮有涨有落，人有盛有衰。

Whoever can keep everlasting youth is a great man.

谁能永远保持青春,谁就是伟大的人。

When young, you took a number of photos and displayed them in the drawing room; when old, you will find they are shown to you because all the scenes of your whole lifetime spread before you and let you omit your memoirs.

年轻时拍下许多照片,摆在客厅给别人看;等到老了发现照片是拍给自己看的。一生的镜头摆在眼前,连写回忆录都省下了。

The art of life is to know how to enjoy a little and to endure much.

生活的艺术就是要学会少享受,多忍受。

Two men look out through the same bars; one sees the mud and another sees the stars.

两个人站在栅栏里向外看,一个人看到的是泥巴,另一个人看到的是星星。

An optimist sees opportunity in every calamity; a pessimist sees a calamity in every opportunity.

乐观者在每场灾难中都看到机遇，悲观者在每次机遇中都看到灾难。

A window of opportunity won't open itself.

机遇之窗不会自己打开。

Losers want security; winners seek opportunity.

失败者寻求安全；成功者寻求机遇。

Youth is the period when one's life is just ready to burst like a bud. It implies an unknown promising future.

青春是一个人生命含苞待放的时期，蕴涵着尚未被认知的、充满希望的未来。

Youth is the period for establishing foundation of the whole life.

青春是奠定一生基础的时期。

Youth and white paper take any impression.

青年像白纸，可以打上任何印记。

One who keeps abreast of the times remains young.

与时俱进的人永远年轻。

Youth for man is the best season, yet it is so short. Once you tear off a leaf from the calendar, you will have the presentiment that a petal of flower of youth has dropped.

青春是人们最美好的季节,而它又是何等短暂。当你撕去日历上的一页,便会预感到青春的花朵凋谢了一瓣。

Get the jewel and you will know its value; only can you know its rarity after the flower of youth wilts.

获得珠宝,方知其价值;青春之花凋谢,才知其珍贵。

Life is a book with invisible characters. Men of sharp eyes can read good lines in it.

生活是本无字书,慧眼人看到精彩词句。

Life, not like a man-made canal, cannot be confined in some defined courses.

生活不是运河,不能禁锢在几条固定的河道里。

Life is like a book, the foolish one reads it carelessly, but the wise one reads it carefully.

人生如书,愚者草草翻过,智者细细品读。

The life of every man is a continued chain of incidents, each link of which hangs upon the former.

每个人的生活是由一连串事件组成的链条,其中的每一环都扣着前一环。

The world is a play that would not be worth seeing if we knew the plot.

世事如戏,知道剧情,那就不值得看了。

Life is a great treasure, and I know how to select the most precious pearls and jewels from it.

人生是大宝藏,我知道如何从这个宝藏里选取最珍贵的珠宝。

Man is a link in the chain of life, which extends through man from the remote past to the indefinite future.

人是生命链的一环,生命链通过人从遥远的过去伸向无限的未来。

Life is like two bottles of beer man must drink: one is sweet, while the other is sour and bitter. After the sweet comes the sour and bitter.

人生就像两瓶必喝的啤酒,一瓶甜,一瓶酸苦,先喝甜的,其后必然是酸苦的。

The meeting of two personalities is like the contact of two chemical substances: if there is any reaction, both are transformed.

两种个性的人相遇如两种化学物质接触:一旦发生反应,双方都将发生改变。

Your life is like a book. The title page is your name; the preface, your introduction to the world. The pages are a daily record of your efforts, trials, pleasures, discouragements. Day by day your thoughts and acts are being inscribed in your book of life. Hour by hour, the record is being made that must stand for all time. One day the word "finish" must be written.

生命就像一本书。扉页写着你的名字,前言是你的简介。正文记录的是你每天的努力、尝试、快乐和沮丧。你的思想和行为都一天天记录在你的生命之书上。生命过程一小时一小时地永远记载其中。有一天,"完"字必须写在上面。

Life is a tragedy when seen in close-up, but a comedy in long-shot.

用特写镜头看,生活是一出悲剧;用长镜头看,生活则是一出喜剧。

The society is a ship, on which everyone must be ready for steering.

社会是一条船,船上的每个人都要准备好掌舵。

Kindness is the golden link by which society is bound together.

善良是将社会联系在一起的金色链条。

A man is a laborer if the job society offers him is of no interest to himself but he is compelled to take it by the necessity of earning a living and supporting his family; a man is a worker if he is personally interested in the job which society pays him to do.

如果一个人对社会提供给他的工作毫无兴趣,只是为了养家糊口而被迫去做,这个人仅仅是一个劳动者;如果一个人对社会提供给他的工作感兴趣,这个人就是一个工作者。

There is no spectator in life.

生活里没有观众。

Life doesn't sell return tickets. Once you set out on this journey, you can't return.

人生不卖往返票,一旦动身无法回。

Life is a novel, which is not its length but its quality that counts.

人生是小说,不在长,而在质量。

A cynic is a man who knows the price of everything and the value of nothing.

玩世不恭者是知道一切东西的价格却不知其价值的人。

You can never plan the future by the past.

——Burke

永远也不能依照过去规划未来。

——伯克

One cannot help being old, but one can resist being aged.

——H. L. Samuel

一个人无法不变老，但可以保持年轻的心态。

——H·L·塞缪尔

A stumble may prevent a fall.

小惩大诫。

Nature never deceives us; it is always us who deceive ourselves.

——Rousseau

大自然永远不会欺骗我们，欺骗我们的往往是我们自己。

——卢梭

A person's soul is like the torch made of hay. If taking action, it must burn per se in advance.

人的心灵好比干草扎成的火把，要发生作用，它必须本身先燃烧。

The utmost pain of life is that nobody needs him.

人生最大的痛苦就是谁也不需要他。

Life is like a play, in which if you act well, you'll be applauded and if you act badly, you'll be cursed.

人生如戏，你演得好便被喝彩，演得坏便被咒骂。

Life is made up of little things.

生活是由许多小事组成的。

Life is not divided into semesters. You don't get summers off and very few employers are interested in helping you find yourself. Do that on your own time.

——Bill Gates

生活不分学期，你没有暑假可以休息，也没有几位雇主乐于帮你发现自我。自己找时间去发现自我吧。

——比尔·盖茨

A man is not old as long as he is seeking something. A man is not old until regrets take the place of dreams.

——J. Barrymore

一个人还有追求，就依然年轻。一旦遗憾取代了梦想，他就成了老人。

——J·巴里摩尔

We are here to add what we can to life, not to get what we can from it.

——W. Osler

我们来到世上是为了尽自己所能给生活增加一些东西，而不是为了从生活中获取我们所能得到的一切。

——W·奥斯勒

The horizon of life is broadened chiefly by the enlargement of the heart.

——H. Black

生活的地平线往往随着心灵的开阔而变得宽广。

——H·布莱克

Life is long if you know how to use it.

—— Seneca

善于利用生命，生命方长久。

—— 塞内加

If you find a path with no obstacles, it probably doesn't lead anywhere interesting.

你所发现的平坦之路也许并不通向任何有趣的地方。

What we once enjoyed and deeply loved we can never lose. For all that we love deeply becomes a part of us.

——Helen Keller

我们曾喜欢并深爱过的与我们相伴终生,因深爱的东西已与我们融为一体。

——海伦·凯勒

Imagination is the beginning of creation. We imagine what we desire; we will what we imagine; and at last we create what we will.

——George Bernard Shaw

创作源于想象,想象源于渴望,所愿源于想象,最终创作源于所愿。

——乔治·萧伯纳

The best bridge between hope and despair is often a good night's sleep.

希望与绝望之间最好的桥梁常常是晚上睡一大觉。

The best way to cheer yourself up is to try to cheer somebody else up.

要使自己振作起来,最好先设法激励他人。

No one person can effect great changes. But many people can bring small changes.

一人难以带来大变化，众人能够带来小变化。

Fate is as if we were dealt a hand of cards. Once we have them, we are free to play them as we choose.

命运就像我们打牌一样。牌一到手，我们就可以有所选择地出牌。

No matter what your age or condition, there are still untapped possibilities within you and new beauty waiting to be born.

无论年龄与条件如何，新的机遇仍存，美好事物依然孕育。

Nobody notices what we do, until we stop doing it.

在我们停下来之前，无人会注意到我们的事业。

Even though one string is broken, the other three will play on. This is life.

即使断了一根弦，其余的三根弦还是要继续演奏。这就是人生。

Life is nothing but a competition to be the criminal rather than the victim.

——Bertrand Russell

人生只是弱肉强食的竞争。

——伯特兰·罗素

Everything ought to be beautiful in a human being: face, dress, soul, and ideas.

——Chekhov

人的一切——面貌、衣着、心灵和思想——都应该是美好的。

——契诃夫

To live is to function. That is all there is in living.

——Holmes

活着就要发挥作用，这就是生活的全部内容。

——霍姆斯

Only when one plunges into the powerful current of the times will one's life shine brilliantly.

一个人只有投身于伟大的时代洪流中，他的生命才会闪耀出光彩。

While there is one untrodden tract for intellect or will, and men are free to think and act, life is worth living.

——A. Austin

只要还有一块知识和意志尚未征服的领域，只要人们还有思考和行动的自由，生活就是值得的。

——A·奥斯汀

The crash of the whole solar and stellar systems could only kill you once.

——Thomas Carlyle

即使整个太阳系和星系崩溃，你也只能死一次。

——托马斯·卡莱尔

To feel that one has a place in life solves half the problem of content.

——G. Woodberry

如果感觉到自己在生活中有了一个位置，满足的问题就解决了一半。

——G·伍德贝利

We should so live and labor in our time that what came to us as seed may go to the next generation as blossom, and what came to us as blossom may go to them as fruit. This is what we mean by progress.

——H. W. Beecher

在当今时代,我们应该这样地生活和工作:使给予我们的种子能在下一代开花;使给予我们的花朵能在下一代结果,这就是我们所说的进步的意义。

——H·W·比彻

It is easier to fight for principles than to live up to them.

——A. E. Stevenson

为原则而斗争容易,达到原则的要求难。

——A·E·史蒂文森

Those who expect to reap the blessings of freedom must undergo the fatigue of supporting it.

——T. Paine

想要享受自由必须竭尽全力维护自由。

——T·潘恩

In nature there are no rewards or punishments; there are consequences.

——H. Annesley Vachell

自然界中没有奖罚,只有结果。

——H·安尼斯利·瓦谢尔

Nobody can run fast enough to escape their own worries. They must be faced, and challenged.

谁也逃脱不了担心的困扰,必须面对并挑战这些困扰。

There is a little madness in every great soul.

伟人都有点疯狂。

To reach the top of the mountain, you must first pass through the foothills.

千里之行,始于脚下。

Giving up doesn't always mean you have failed. Sometimes it is a sign that you are strong enough to let go.

放弃并非总意味着失败,有时意味着你足够强大。

Ideas pull the trigger, but instinct loads the gun.

——Marquis

思想扣动扳机,然而是直觉装上子弹。

——马尔奎斯

Any man can make mistakes, but only an idiot persists in his error.

——Cicero

任何人都可能犯错误,但只有傻瓜才坚持错误。

——西塞罗

Accept change, but make sure that your core values are unchangeable.

接受改变,但核心价值观一定不能变。

Finish each task; if you rush from one to another, you are setting your brain to high alert, as if you were being chased by a predator.

事情一件件了结,不要匆忙干一件又一件,让大脑高度紧张,好像被猎食者追逐。

Find within yourself a place of stillness, through mindful meditation. You'll find that after a while, your attention span, concentration, and memory will improve.

通过沉思冥想让自己沉静下来,很快就会发现注意力、集中力和记忆力都会改善。

Meditation helps concentration, both on the small and great tasks of life.

沉思有助于集中精力解决生活中的大小事情。

I ask not for a lighter burden, but for broader shoulders.

我祈求更宽的肩膀,不祈求更轻的负担。

Man can only be free through mastery of himself.

——S. E. Morison

只有通过掌握自己,才能使自己得到解放。

——S·E·莫里森

Life is a great big canvas, and you should throw all the paint you can on it.

人生是一幅大画布,你应该努力绘出绚丽多彩的画面。

Life is a horse, and either you ride it or it rides you.

人生像一匹马,你不驾驭它,它便驾驭你。

Life means struggle.

生活就是斗争。

Towering genius disdains a beaten path. He seeks regions hitherto unexplored.

——Abraham Lincoln

卓越的天才不屑走他人走过的路,他要寻找迄今未开拓的地域。

——亚伯拉罕·林肯

Life would be too smooth if it had no rubs in it.

生活若无波折,就会过于平淡无奇。

Life can only be understood backwards, but it must be lived forwards.

——Kierkegaard

向后看才能理解生活,但生活必须向前进。

——克尔凯郭尔

There's only one corner of the universe you can be certain of improving, and that's your own self.

——Huxley

宇宙中只有一介之地你肯定可以改善,那就是你自己。

——赫胥黎

Life is just a series of trying to make up your mind.

——T. Fuller

生活就是一系列下决心的过程。

——T·富勒

Fear not that the life shall come to an end, but rather fear that it shall never have a beginning.

——J. H. Newman

不要害怕你的生活将要结束,应该担心你的生活永远不会真正开始。

——J·H·纽曼

Beggars cannot be choosers.

——Heywood

行乞者无选择。

——希伍德

The unexamined life is not worth living.

——Socrates

浑浑噩噩的生活不值得过。

——苏格拉底

Part of being human is to rise above your own particular concerns and see the entire picture.

做人不要囿于私事，要纵览全局。

A new idea is delicate. It can be killed by a sneer or a yawn; it can be stabbed to death by a quip and worried to death by a frown on the right man's brow.

——Charles Brower

新想法非常脆弱，可能被一声耻笑、一个呵欠和一句嘲讽扼杀，或者因某权威人士的蹙眉而郁郁而终。

——查尔斯·布劳尔

Do something every day for no other reason than you would rather not do it, so that when the hour of dire need draws nigh, it may find you not unnerved and untrained to stand the test.

——William James

只因为之总比不为好，每天做些事。时机一到，便可精神抖擞，训练有素，经受考验。

——威廉·詹姆斯

Do what you have to do, so you can do what you want to do.

先不得已而为之，而后才能为所欲为。

Do not be overwhelmed by busy thoughts; learn to manage them, not through banishing them, but simply by letting them pass by you.

不要让各种想法搅昏头，学会控制这些想法，不是放弃，而是直接不想。

To believe in one's dreams is to spend all of one's life asleep.

沉湎于自己的梦想就是把一生的时间花在睡觉上。

A mirror can only help you see the stain on your face; and wipe it off, you have to rely on yourself.

镜子只能帮你看到脸上的污点；而要擦掉它，还得靠你自己。

You're the captain of the ship called you. You're setting the course, the speed, and you're out there on the bridge, steering.

你是自己这艘船的船长；你设定航线、速度，而且你就在船桥上掌舵。

Optimism is the faith that leads to achievement. Nothing can be done without hope and confidence.

——Helen Keller

乐观主义能带来成就。没有希望与信心,将一事无成。

——海伦·凯勒

Youth is like gold, with which you can make what you want to make.

青春就像黄金,可用来随意塑造。

Chance favors those in motion.

机遇不青睐懒惰者。

If life is a grindstone, use it to sharpen your wits.

如果生活是一块磨石,那就用它去磨砺你的智慧吧。

The orbit of life is unforeknowable, so no one can finish his autobiography in advance.

人生的轨道无法预知,谁也不能事先写好自传。

Youth is the period when one's life is just ready to burst like a bud. It implies an unknown promising future.

青春是生命中含苞待放的时期，它蕴含着未知的、充满希望的未来。

The only place success comes before work is in the dictionary.

没有奋斗便成功是天方夜谭。

He that would have fruit must climb the tree.

要想吃果子必须爬树摘。

The value of life lies not in the length of days, but in the use we make of them.

生命的价值不在于能活多少天，而在于如何使用这些日子。

There isn't any value in life itself, whose value lies in how to use it.

生命本身没有任何价值，其价值在于如何利用生命。

Life is like chess. The loss of one step makes the loss of all. Even life is no better than chess, for it has no more chess and cannot regret.

人生就像下棋，一步走错，全盘皆输。甚至人生还不如下棋，因为它不可能再来一局，也不能悔棋。

Life is like music. It must be composed by ear, feeling and instinct, not by rule.

人生如一首乐曲，要用乐感、感情和直觉去谱写，而非按规则。

When we do the best we can, we never know what miracle is wrought in our life, or in the life of another.

——Helen Keller

我们尽力而为，从不知道能给我们的生活或者另一个人的生活带来什么奇迹。

——海伦·凯勒

Fortune befriends the bold.

财富青睐大胆的。

All things are difficult before they are easy.

凡事先难后易。

All life is a chance. So take it!

——Dale Carnegie

人生就是一次机遇，抓住这个机遇！

——戴尔·卡耐基

Life is not a spectacle or a feast. It is a predicament.

生活不是美景，也不是盛宴，而是困境。

The law of life should not be the competition of acquisitiveness, but cooperation, the good of each contributing to the good of all.

生活的法则不应是看谁得的多，而应是合作，是奉献。

Life is at least only a children's game, Yet the game must be played conscientiously.

生活算是一个儿童游戏，但这个游戏必须认真去玩。

Humor is a lifebuoy in the waves of life.

幽默是生活波涛中的救生圈。

Life is an ocean, where in only men of strong will reach the destination.

生活就像海洋，只有意志坚强的人，才能到达彼岸。

The most important in life is not to remember but to forget.

人生最重要的不是记住，而是遗忘。

Our life style is like an oil painting, which we cannot see its beauty unless in a far distance.

我们的生活方式就像一幅油画：如不远观，难见其美。

Life is like a fable, which is measured not by its length but by its content.

生命如同寓言，其价值不以其长短而以其内容来衡量。

Death comes to all, but great achievements raise a monument which shall endure until the sun grows old.

死亡无人幸免，但丰功伟绩会立起一座永恒的纪念碑。

To have a grievance is to have a purpose in life.

不满意，就等于有了人生目标。

迎难而上

Honor your challenges, for those spaces that you label as dark are actually there to bring you more light.

尊重你遇到的挑战，那些被你称为黑暗的地方实际上能带给你更多光明。

A little boy was asked how he learned to skate. “By getting up every time I fell down,” he answered.

——David Seabury

“每次摔倒后，爬起来。”小孩子被问及如何学会滑冰的时候说道。

——大卫·西伯里

Don’t be too hard on yourself. Criticizing natural emotions, like anger or jealousy, will only increase feelings of frustration. Instead, try to ask yourself, why do I feel like this?

不要苛求自己。对自然情感如愤怒或嫉妒的自责只会增加挫败感。解决的办法最好是思考一下为什么会有这种感情的产生。

Courage is not the towering oak that sees storms come and go; it is the fragile blossom that opens in the snow.

勇气不是经历暴风雨的参天橡树，而是冰天雪地中绽放的柔弱花朵。

Cease to struggle and you cease to live.

—— Thomas Carlyle

停止奋斗，虽生犹死。

——托马斯·卡莱尔

I will overcome myself like a lion.

—— Beethoven

我要像狮子一样战胜自己。

—— 贝多芬

A strong man will struggle with the storms of fate.

—— Thomas Edison

强者愿意搏击命运。

——托马斯·爱迪生

When you lose, don't lose heart.

失败，但不失去信心。

Man cannot discover new oceans unless he has courage to lose sight of the shore.

—— A. Gide

只有鼓起勇气，离岸远航，才能进入新的海域。

——A·纪德

A man can fail many times, but he isn't a failure until he begins to blame somebody else.

一个人可以失败许多次,但只要他没有开始责怪别人,他还不算是一个失败者。

Cowards die many times before their deaths.

——Julius Caesar

怯懦者在真正死亡之前,已死过多次。

——朱利尤斯·恺撒

A certain amount of care or pain or trouble is necessary for every man at all times. A ship without ballast is unstable and will not go straight.

——Arthur Schopenhauer

每个时代的每个人都需要一定的忧愁、痛苦或烦恼,如同船只没有压舱物就难以平稳致远。

——阿瑟·叔本华

There are a lot ways to become a failure, but never taking a chance is the most unsuccessful.

失败原因有多种,坐失良机首当其冲。

Falling down doesn't make you a failure, but staying down does.

失败不在于摔倒,而在于倒地不起。

It is only to turn the mood of complaining surroundings into the urge of making progress that ensures success.

只有把抱怨环境的心情化为上进的力量,才能保证成功。

Failures are divided into people who thought and never did, and people who did and never thought.

失败者分为两种人:一种是只想不做,一种是只做不想。

He that would make sure of success should keep his passion cool, and his expectation low.

要想成功,头脑要冷静,期望值要低。

If you mess up, it's not your parents' fault, so don't whine about our mistakes, learn from them.

——Bill Gates

陷入困境不是父母的过错，所以不要尖声抱怨，要从中吸取教训。

——比尔·盖茨

Meet success like a gentleman and disaster like a man.

——Fredrich Edwin Smith Birkenhead

以绅士风度面对成功，以勇士气概正视困难。

——弗里德里希·埃德温·史密斯·伯肯黑德

Man errs as long as he strives.

——Goethe

只要进取就会有失误。

——歌德

The failures and reverses which await men—and one after another sadden the brow of youth—add a dignity to the prospect of human life, which no Arcadian success would do.

——Henry David Thoreau

年轻时经历的一次次失败和挫折，让人蹙额，但给未来人生增添的尊严是一帆风顺的成功所不能给予的。

——亨利·大卫·梭罗

A man who fears suffering is already suffering from what he fears.

——Michel E. Montaigne

害怕痛苦的人已经受到其恐惧带来的心理煎熬。

——迈克尔·E·蒙田

There is nothing permanent in life, except change.

生活中没有一成不变,只有变化一成不变。

Lookers-on see most of the game.

——Smedley

旁观者清。

——斯梅德利

Life is constantly pounding you from the outside with millions of hammer blows, but you have the last word as to how those blows will change you.

人生经常有来自外部的无数打击,但这些打击如何影响你,最终决定权在你手里。

Happiness is beneficial for the body, but it is grief that develops the powers of the mind.

——Marcel Proust

愉快有益于健康,但只有悲伤才能培养心灵的力量。

——马塞尔·普鲁斯特

Forget mistakes. Forget failure. Forget everything except what you're going to do now and do it.

忘却错误,忘却失败,忘却一切,只要记住你现在要做的事情,并着手去做。

Enduring disappointment in life, with a good grace, is a way of overcoming it, and will, at the very least, earn you your self-respect.

优雅地忍受生活中的失望,有助于消除失望,至少赢得自尊。

The beauty of the soul shines out when a man bears with composure one heavy mischance after another, not because he does not feel them, but because he is a man of high and heroic temper.

——Aristotle

一个人泰然自若地承受接踵而至的灾难,并非反应迟钝,而是勇敢坚韧,其美丽心灵在危难中熠熠闪光。

——亚里士多德

Pressure makes diamonds.

重压之下出钻石。

Failure is the mother of success.

失败是成功之母。

Misfortune is the prelude to the accomplishments.

厄运是成就的前奏。

We never stop making mistakes; and we must never stop learning from them.

我们从未停止犯错,所以必须永远吸取教训。

The real test is not whether you avoid this failure, because you won't. It's whether you let it harden and shame you into inaction, or whether you learn from it; whether you choose to persevere. Barack Obama

真正的考验不是你是否避免失败,因为失败不可避免,而是你为失败感到麻木、耻辱并放弃努力,还是吸取教训,继续努力。

It's a little like wrestling a gorilla. You don't quit when you're tired — you quit when the gorilla is tired.

——Robert Strauss

就像与大猩猩摔跤，累了也不能跑；大猩猩累了，你再跑。

——罗伯特·斯特拉斯

Fear is like fire: if controlled, it will help you; if uncontrolled, it will rise up and destroy you.

——John F. Milburn

恐惧如火，加以控制，有益于你；如果失控，大火蔓延，造成毁灭。

——约翰·F·米尔本

Adversity introduces a man to himself.

——Albert Einstein

逆境让人了解自己。

——阿尔伯特·爱因斯坦

The longest day has an end.

——Howell

最难过的日子也有尽头。

——贺韦尔

Fear cannot be without hope, nor hope without fear.

——Baruch Spinoza

恐惧离不开希望,希望也离不开恐惧。

——巴鲁克·斯宾诺莎

In this world there is always danger for those who are afraid of it.

——George Bernard Shaw

对害怕危险的人来说,这个世界总是危险的。

——乔治·萧伯纳

Don't waste life in doubts and fears.

——Thomas Carlyle

不要在怀疑和恐惧中浪费生命。

——托马斯·卡莱尔

Life is an ocean, wherein only men of strong will reach the destination.

生活就像海洋,只有意志坚强的人,才能到达彼岸。

Our greatest glory is not in never failing, but in rising up every time we fail.

我们最大的光荣不是从不失败，而是每次失败后都能站起来。

Our destiny offers not the cup of despair, but the chalice of opportunity. So let us seize it, not in fear, but in gladness.

——Richard Nixon

命运给予我们的不是失望之苦水，而是机遇之美酒。因此，我们要毫无畏惧、满心愉悦地去把握命运。

——理查德·尼克松

No pain, no palm; no thorns, no throne; no gall, no glory; no cross, no crown.

没有辛劳，就没有收获；没有荆棘，就没有王座；没有磨难，就没有辉煌；没有苦难，就没有王冠。

Never bend your head. Always hold it high. Look at the world straight in the face.

千万别低下你的头，永远高昂着头，勇敢地正视世界。

The one who lies on the ground will never fall down.

躺在地上的人永远不会摔倒。

Every successful person had gone through much unsuccessful time.

每个成功者都经历过许多不成功的岁月。

Something attempted, something done.

——Longfellow

有所尝试,就有所作为。

——朗费罗

Adversity is the first access to truth.

逆境是达到真理的第一条道路。

Nothing in life is to be feared. It is only to be understood.

——Marie Curie

生活中没有什么可怕的东西,只有需要理解的东西。

——玛丽·居里

Man's extremity is God's opportunity.

绝境是上帝给予的良机。

When you succeed, the most uncommon is to have no enemy; when you fail, the most uncommon is to have friends.

成功时,最难得的是没有敌人;失败时,最难得的是还有朋友。

Being defeated is often a temporary condition. Giving up is what makes it permanent.

失败通常是暂时的,放弃则是永久失败。

It is the original color of a fighter that he strives to do good after censured.

受到指责依然努力做好事,是奋斗者的本色。

Even after the victory, you should buckle the belts on your helmet and armor.

即使胜利后,也要扣紧盔甲上的带子。

We may pass violets looking for roses. We may pass contentment looking for victory.

我们可能会走过紫罗兰去寻找玫瑰,心满意足了,可能还会去寻找胜利。

Perseverance is not a long race; it is many short races one after another.

坚持并非一次长跑,而是一次接一次的无数短跑。

Only the successful person can have the power to sweetly recall the benefits that the tribulation ever brought them.

只有成功人士才有权甜蜜地回忆磨难带给他们的好处。

The real world is not easy to live in. It is rough; it is slippery. Without the most clear-eyed adjustments we fall and get crushed. A man must stay sober: not always, but most of the time.

生活在现实世界非易事,道路坎坷又湿滑。若非瞪大眼睛随时应变,就会摔倒而遭碾压。必须保持清醒:不用时刻清醒,而是大部分时间清醒。

Man can be destroyed, but not defeated.

人可以被毁灭,但不能被打败。

Courage comes and goes. Hold on for the next supply.

—— Thomas Merton

勇气时大时小,坚持再次鼓起勇气。

——托马斯·默顿

善用时间

Time is a great teacher, but unfortunately it kills all its pupils.

——Hector Berlioz

时间是个伟大老师,不幸的是所有的学生都被其杀死。

——埃克托·柏辽兹

The present is the necessary result of all the past, and the cause of all the future.

现在是一切过去的必然结果,也是一切未来的起因。

A man who dares to waste one hour of time has not discovered the value of life.

——Charles Darwin

连一小时都浪费的人是没有发现生命的价值。

——查尔斯·达尔文

A day dawns, quite like other days; in it a single hour comes, quite like other hours; but in that day and in that hour the chance of a lifetime faces us.

天亮了,一如其他日子;一小时来了,一如其他小时,但就在这一天、这一小时,人生的机遇来了。

Life is so brief and time is fleeting. Grasp it and it will be an opportunity; depict it and it will be a rainbow.

生命如此短暂,光阴飞逝如箭。抓住它,它就是机会;描绘它,它就是彩虹。

Yesterday is but today's memory, and tomorrow is today's dream.

——Khalil Gibran

昨天已成为今天的记忆,明天是今天的梦想。

——哈利勒·纪伯伦

Life is short, so don't waste a second of it!

生命短暂,分秒必争。

Today is the first day of the rest of your life.

今天是你余生的第一天。

Look at everything always as though you were seeing it either for the first or last time.

——Betty Smith

看待每一件事情,都当作人生第一次见到或者最后一次见到。

——贝蒂·史密斯

Today is the tomorrow we worried about yesterday.

今天是我们昨天担心的明天。

Even a clock that has stopped is right twice a day.

即使钟表停了，一天也有两次表示的时间是正确的。

Don't sigh with regret over the passed time, and you should face up to the time sneaking away.

不要为已消逝的年华惋惜，而应面对正在匆匆溜走的时光。

Youth is half the battle.

年轻是战役的一半。

Youth gives us love and rose; age still leaves us friends and wine.

青春赋予我们爱情和玫瑰，岁月则留给我们朋友和美酒。

Flowers are in bloom in summer; people are in their prime in youth.

花在夏天绽放，人在年轻时兴旺。

Time is the most impartial, for it gives everyone twenty four hours; time is the most partial, for it doesn't give twenty-four hours to anyone.

时间最公正,因为它给每个人都是 24 小时;时间又最偏心,因为并非任何人都得到 24 小时。

Remember that time is money. Dost thou love life? Then don't squander time, for that's the stuff life is made of.

记住,时间就是金钱。你热爱生命吗?那就别浪费时间,因为生命是由时间构成的。

Time is a bird forever on the wing.

时间是一只永远飞翔的小鸟。

Punctuality is the politeness of kings.

守时是最大的礼貌。

Time is the only capital for those who possess nothing but intelligence.

对于除了聪明才智外一无所有的人,时间是唯一的资本。

Every day is a new beginning; every sunset is merely the latest milestone on a voyage that never ends.

每一天都是新的开始；每一次日落不过是永无尽头的航程中最新的一个里程碑。

Wasting time is robbing oneself.

浪费时间，就是掠夺自己。

In our expenditure the item that costs most is time.

在我们的消费中，时间是最昂贵的一项。

A man, who wastes all his lifetime, is to throw out gold without buying anything.

虚度一生，就像抛出黄金而一无所获。

Time always makes its customers in debt. It lends them every minute and second, but asks them to pay their age in return.

时光总是让它的顾客欠账，它借给他们分秒，却要他们以年岁偿还。

The future is exchanged with the present.

未来是用现在换来的。

By thinking anxiously about the future, we forget the present, such that we live neither for the present nor the future.

我们急切憧憬未来,忘记了现在,以致我们既不是为了现在也不是为了将来而活着。

Like coral insects multitudinous, the minutes are whereof our life is made.

像无数的珊瑚虫聚成了珊瑚,分分秒秒构成我们的一生。

Every moment is of infinite worth, for it is the representative of a whole eternity.

每一时刻都有无限的价值,因为它是永恒的代表。

Time is something man is always trying to kill, but which ends in killing him.

人们打发时间,最终被时间打发。

Time that strengthens friendships weakens love.

时间会增进友谊,却会削弱爱情。

Times flies so fast that it makes no distinction between day and night.

时光飞逝，不舍昼夜。

Time is like the water in the sponge. It can still be squeezed out if you like to.

时间，就像海绵里的水，只要愿挤，总还是有的。

He who will not when he may, when he will he shall have nay.

可为时不想为，想为时已不可为。

Never leave that until tomorrow , which you can do today.

今天能做的事不要拖到明天。

Don't dawdle away your time, or your hair will soon turn gray. Then you will moan and mourn in vain.

莫等闲，白了少年头，空悲切。

The value of a man's life increases with the fact that he really knows how to make full use of his time.

真正懂得充分利用时间的人，他的生命价值也会因此增加。

Time and tide wait for no man. In an instant the black hair might become silvery white.

光景不待人，须臾黑发成银丝。

Yesterday is an invalid cheque, tomorrow is a term bill, but today is the only cash you own, so you should seize it intelligently.

昨天是一张过期支票，明天是一张期票，而今天则是你唯一拥有的现金，所以应当巧妙把握。

Many, while walking forth and back on one road, have to make way for those valuing time and let them go ahead.

当许多人在一条路上徘徊不前时，不得不让开一条路，让那些珍惜时间的人赶到前面去。

Time is the most fair and reasonable—it never gives more to anyone. To hard workers, time leaves clusters of fruits, while to the idlers, time leaves only grey hair and empty hands.

时间最公平合理，它从不多给谁一分。时间给勤劳者留下串串果实；给懒惰者只能留下一头白发、两手空空。

Time is a mansion which even cannot be copied by almighty God.

时间是一座连万能的上帝也无法复制的大厦。

Man has no port and time no shore. Life passes as water.

人无港口，时无岸，时光如水不复返。

Time and thinking melt the strongest grief.

时间和思考化解最大的忧愁。

Time passes slowly for the man who allows himself to be bored.

不愿摆脱厌烦，时间过得很慢。

Make the most of your life. You may have less time left than you think.

充分利用生命，你会发现时间比预料的要紧迫。

Time drops in delay, like a candle burnt out.

——William Butler Yeats

时间点点滴滴地消失,犹如蜡烛慢慢燃尽。

——威廉·巴特勒·叶芝

The best way to suppose what may come is to remember what is past.

——George Halifax

推测将要发生什么,最好是记住已经发生了什么。

——乔治·哈利法克斯

Lost wealth may be replaced by industry, lost knowledge by study, lost health by temperance of medicine, but lost time is gone forever.

——Samuel Smiles

勤奋可挣回失去的财富,学习可弥补忘掉的知识,适度治疗可恢复失去的健康,但是光阴逝去则永不复返。

——塞缪尔·斯迈尔斯

Yesterday's just a memory, tomorrow is never what it's supposed to be.

——Bob Dylan

昨天已成为回忆，没人知道明天会发生什么。

——鲍勃·迪伦

Weep no more, no sigh, nor groan. Sorrow calls no time that's gone.

——John Fletcher

别哭泣，别叹息，别呻吟；悲伤唤不回流逝的时光。

——约翰·弗莱切

Today is Yesterday's pupil.

今天是昨天的学生。

Even very short periods of time add up to all useful hours I need, if I plunge in without delay.

——John Erskine

马上投入工作，时间再短，积累起来就成为所需要的有用时间。

——约翰·厄斯金

There is an important trick in this time-using formula: you must get into your work quickly.

——John Erskine

利用时间有个重要的诀窍：必须迅速投入工作。

——约翰·厄斯金

No one can call back yesterday.

昨日不会重现。

Ordinary people merely think how they shall spend their time; man of talent tries to use it.

普通人只考虑如何消磨时光，有才能的人则是设法利用时间。

We always have time enough, if we will but use it aright.

只要我们能善用时间，就永远不愁时间不够用。

Time cures all things.

时间是医治一切创伤的良药。

Time tries all.

路遥知马力，日久见人心。

Time is a bird forever on the wing.

时间是一只永远展翅飞翔的鸟。

One cannot put back the clock.

时钟不能倒转。

Lost time is never found again.

岁月既往,谁也找不回。

The simple life is not necessarily living in a cabin, cultivating beans. It is refusing to let our lives be frittered away by detail.

——W. Richard

简朴的生活并不一定要住在木屋里,种瓜种豆,而是不为琐事浪费生命。

——W·理查德

Don't put off till tomorrow what should be done today.

今日事,今日毕。

One today is worth two tomorrows.

一个今天胜似两个明天。

An hour in the morning is worth two in the evening.

——Benjamin Franklin

一日之计在于晨。

——本杰明·富兰克林

What may be done at any time will be done at no time.

我生待明日,万事成蹉跎。

I am a slow walker, but I never walk backwards.

——Abraham Lincoln

我走得很慢,但是我从不后退。

——亚伯拉罕·林肯

A day is a miniature of eternity.

一天是永恒的缩影。

Old age is like everything else. To make a success of it, you have got to start young.

——Fred Astaire

欲求老年成功,须从年轻时开始。世上万事,都是如此。

——弗瑞德·阿斯泰厄

To him that does everything in its proper time, one day is worth three.

办事抓时机,一日抵三日。

To choose time is to save time.

——Francis Bacon

选择时间就是节省时间。

——弗朗西斯·培根

Until we can manage TIME, we can manage nothing else.

会管理时间才会管理一切。

You are not born for fame if you don't know the value of time.

——Peter F. Drucker

如果不知道时间的价值,你注定难以有所成就。

——彼得·F·德卢克

Live as long as you may, the first twenty years are the longest half of your life.

——Southey

不管你活得多久,头二十年都是你一生中最长的那一半。

——骚塞

To save time is to lengthen life.

节约时间就是延长生命。

Today's today. Tomorrow, we may be ourselves gone down the drain of eternity.

——Euripides

今天就是今天，明天我们就可能消失于永恒之中。

——欧里庇得斯

Time past cannot be called back again.

时间不能倒流。

Nothing in the world is more valuable than time; nothing in the world is more extravagant than the waste of time.

天下最可宝贵的莫如时日；天下最奢侈的莫如耗时。

The value of a man's life increases with the fact that he really knows how to make full use of his time.

真正懂得充分利用时间的人，他的生命价值也会因此增加。

Busy bees never feel sad about time.

辛勤的蜜蜂永远不会对时间感到悲哀。

Time has three kinds of paces; the future comes slowly, the present flies like an arrow, and the past stands still.

时间有三种步伐：未来姗姗来迟，现在飞逝如箭，过去静立不动。

Nobody can make the clock strike the hour passed.

谁也无法让时钟敲响已经逝去的钟点。

A miser speaks of money as his lifeblood; an assiduous person looks on time as his life.

守财奴说金钱是命根，勤奋者将时间看作生命。

The future is like heaven—everyone exalts it but no one wants to go there now.

未来像天堂——每个人都赞美它，但谁也不想现在就去。

Time is like a flowing stream. It is better for you to forge ahead with it quickly than just on the bank to watch it lapsing away.

时光像一条潺潺流动的小溪。与其坐在岸边看它流逝，不如快步行进随它向前。

The best prophet of the future is the past.

对未来最好的预言就是过去。

Better not to fancy something when the evening sun sets, but to be absorbed in work when the morning sun rises.

最好不要在夕阳西下时幻想什么,而要在旭日东升时投入工作。

A man who is virtually busy has no time to have a bee in his head.

真正忙碌的人不会去胡思乱想。

You can clutch the past so tightly to your chest that it leaves your arms too full to embrace the present.

你将过去抱得太紧,就会腾不出手来拥抱现在。

In all criticism, time is the greatest, most correct and intelligent.

在所有的批评中,最伟大、最正确、最明智的是时间。

No man is rich enough to buy back his past.

再富有的人也买不回自己的过去。

If we quarrel between the past and the present, we shall find that we have lost the future.

如果纠缠在过去和现在之间,就会发现我们失去了未来。

No birds are in last year's nest.

去年的巢里不留鸟。

Fools expect tomorrow; wise men use tonight.

愚者指望明天,智者利用今晚。

Procrastination is the thief of time.

拖延是时间大盗。

In the sea of time, diligent people have a good trip, those who do nothing all day strike a reef everywhere.

在时间的海洋里,勤奋者一帆风顺,无所事事者处处触礁。

We must use time as a tool, not as a couch.

我们一定要把时间当作工具,而不要当作睡椅。

Take time to work, for time is the price of success.

花时间去工作吧,因为时间是成功的代价。

Take time to think, for time is the source of power.

花时间去思考吧,因为时间是力量的源泉。

Time is everything for all of us.

对我们大家,时间就是一切。

Take time to laugh, for time is the music of the soul.

花时间去欢笑吧,因为时间是心灵的音乐。

Time is the healer of all conflicts.

时间是一切冲突的治愈者。

Time lost may be repented but never be recalled.

失去时间可以后悔,但无法追回。

Those who are poor at using time always complain of passing time as fast as lightning.

不善于运用时间的人,总是为时间的快如闪电而抱怨。

Youth looks ahead, old age looks back, and middle age looks tired.

青年往前看,老年向后看,中年疲惫不堪。

We should calculate the time by the heartbeat.

我们应该用心跳来计算光阴。

Please listen to the words of time with attention, for time is the wisest counselor.

请聚精会神倾听时间说话,因为时间是最英明的顾问。

Nothing makes a person more productive than the last minute.

只有最后一分钟才使人多产。

If you cherish every minute of your time, each minute will become a miniature of eternity.

如果你珍惜每一瞬间,每一瞬间也就成了小小的永恒。

It is murder wasting other people's time; it is a slow suicide wasting one's own time.

浪费别人的时间是谋杀，浪费自己的时间则是慢性自杀。

There is no other misfortune that can be compared with the loss of time.

没有一种不幸可与失去时间相比。

There is no time like the present.

最好的时间就是现在。

Time is the soul of the world.

时间是世界的灵魂。

Time gives the visionary people pain, but brings the creative happiness.

时间给空想者痛苦，却给创造者带来幸福。

I wasted time, and now time will waste me.

荒废时间，时间也会让你荒废。

He who gains time gains all things.

赢得时间，就赢得了一切。

Time is the soil of all achievements in the world.

时间是世界上一切成就的土壤。

Time envelopes and visualizes everything.

时间遮盖一切,也显现一切。

If you cry for missing the sun, you will miss all stars.

为错过太阳而哭泣,也会错过星星。

Time flows, like a quiet water, without any fissures, and wrinkles, calmly and leisurely, as if it is so forever.

时间流逝,像平静的河水,既没有裂痕,也没有波纹,从容不迫,仿佛永远如此。

Nothing belongs to us except time.

除了时间,什么也不属于我们。

Since thou art not sure of a minute, throw not away an hour.

既然连一分钟都把握不住,那就别虚掷一小时。

Time is the archives of history.

时间是历史的档案。

Time is the most sacred gift. Every day is a small life.

时间是最神圣的礼物。每一天都是一小段人生。

Time is a loan that cannot be returned even if the borrower is as good as his word.

时间是再守信用者也还不上的贷款。

Time is the angel of mankind.

时间是人类的天使。

You may delay, but time will not.

你可以晚点,但时间不会。

Grasp today better than two tomorrows.

把握今天胜过两个明天。

To sensible men, every day is a day of reckoning.

对明智者来说,每一天都是要计算盈亏的。

A loafer always has the correct time.

游手好闲的人总有正好的时间。

Time, grasp it and it will be gold, or it will be running water.
时间,抓住就是金子,否则就是流水。

What cannot afford to be wasted is time.
最浪费不起的是时间。

Time works wonders.
时间创造奇迹。

Time is the most rigorous jude.
时间是最严厉的法官。

Look to this day, for yesterday is but a dream.
关注今天,昨天不过是一场梦。

Diligence is the master of time; laziness the slave.
勤奋是时间的主人,懒惰是时间的奴隶。

Time is enough, but always proves little enough.
时间充裕,用起来常显不足。

What I do today is important because I am exchanging a day of my life for it.

我今天做的事很重要,因为我为它付出了一天的生命代价。

You cannot have two forenoons in the same day.

同一天里不会有两个上午。

I am not afraid of tomorrow, for I have seen yesterday and I love today.

我不怕明天,因为我目睹了昨天并热爱今天。

Time is a soundless file.

时间是无声的锉刀。

One must wait until the evening to see how splendid the day has been.

人往往等到夜晚来临,才明白白天是多么辉煌。

Time floats with the current and life sails against the current.

时间顺流而下,生活逆水行舟。

善于处世

Laughter is the shortest distance between two people.

——Victor Borge

欢笑拉近两人距离。

——维克多·博尔格

Be nice to nerds. Chances are you'll end up working for one.

——Bill Gates

礼貌对待乏味的人,有可能到头来你会为一个乏味的人工作。

—— 比尔·盖茨

You can never be overdressed, so choose your clothes wisely.

——Mike Matera

着装不可过分,择装要明智。

——迈克·马德拉

A friendship founded on a business is better than business founded on a friendship.

——John Davision Rockefeller

建立在商务基础上的友谊胜过建立在友谊基础上的商务。

——约翰·戴维森·洛克菲勒

A drop of honey catches more flies than a bucket of poison.

一滴蜜比一桶毒药捉住的苍蝇还多。

When a man is wrapped up in himself he makes a pretty little package.

——John Ruskin

只顾自己难成大器。

——约翰·罗斯金

Be good to the ones who love you and be good to yourself. You will be rich beyond your wildest dreams!

——Freewind

爱人爱己,你难以想象自己多富有!

——弗里温德

When you make peace with yourself, you can be in peace with the rest of the world. If you can recognize the spirit in yourself, you can recognize the spirit in everyone, and then you find it natural to be kind and well disposed to all.

——Remez Sasson

心态平和,就能与世人和睦相处;能赏识自己的心灵,就能欣赏他人的心灵;那么,你自然会对别人和善友好。

——雷米兹·萨松

Goodness and being kind do not necessarily point to weakness. When you are good, you can also be strong.

——Remez Sasson

善良、友善待人并不表明你软弱。和善也可以显示坚强。

——雷米兹·萨松

Steadfastly remain humble. The rewards for humility are vast and far-reaching.

——Kurt Lee Hurley

始终保持谦逊,谦逊会给你带来长久的丰厚回报。

——库尔特·李·赫尔利

Gratitude is the fairest blossom that springs from the soul.

——Henry Ward Beecher

感恩是心灵绽放的最美花朵。

——亨利·沃德·比奇

Pardon all but thyself.
宽恕所有人,只是别宽恕自己。

There is more pleasure in loving than in being loved.
施人以爱比受人之爱的乐趣多。

A friend's frown is better than a fool's smile.
朋友对你皱眉,胜过傻瓜对你微笑。

A bird is known by its note and a man by his talk.
闻声知鸟名,闻言见人心。

Money and good manners make the gentleman.
财产与修养成就绅士。

Nurture passes nature.
教养胜过天性。

Civility costs nothing.
礼貌不费分文。

Birth is much, but breeding is more.
出身固然重要,教养更为重要。

Life is so short but there is time enough for courtesy.

人生再短也有足够的时间讲礼貌。

None but the well-bred man knows how to confess a fault, or acknowledge himself in an error.

唯有有教养者方知如何承认错误,或承认自己的过失。

Friendship cannot live with ceremony, nor without civility.

友谊不能有客套,但也离不开礼貌。

The hardest thing children face today is learning good manners without seeing any.

今天孩子所面对的最大问题就是学习礼仪但却无所效仿。

A smart coat is a good letter of introduction.

得体着装就是一封绝好的介绍信。

Apparel makes the man.

人靠衣装。

A good face is a letter of recommendation.

好的相貌就是一封推荐信。

Image does speak volumes. Your overall appearance, facial expression, age, gender, and body language compose a good part of the message you present to another person at your first meeting.

——Jeff Davidson

形象的确能传递信息。和别人初次见面时,整体形象、面部表情、年龄、性别和肢体语言都能向对方传递大量的信息。

——杰弗·戴维森

We think according to nature. We speak according to rules. We act according to custom.

——Francis Bacon

我们凭着天性思考,依据规则说话,按照习俗行事。

——弗朗西斯·培根

Cut your morning DEVOTIONS into your personal grooming. You would not go out to work with a dirty face. Why start the day with the face of your soul unwashed?

——Robert A. Cook

早晨花点时间为自己梳洗妆饰。不要蓬头垢面去上班。为什么要精神不振地开始一天呢?

——罗伯特·A·库克

A best friend is someone you can tell your hopes and dreams to and know they won't laugh.

最好的朋友就是可以与之谈希望和梦想,而你知道不会被嘲笑的人。

A true friend is someone who likes you and doesn't want anything from you.

真正的朋友是喜欢你但对你无所图的人。

If you want to make friends, don't try to impress people with how interesting you are. Instead, listen to them, and find out how interesting they are.

交朋友,不要努力取悦于人,而是善于倾听,发现对方是多么有趣。

The best way to destroy an enemy is to make him a friend.

——Abraham Lincoln

消灭敌人最好的办法是化敌为友。

——亚伯拉罕·林肯

Some people are loners. They prefer to live separately from others. But however independent they are, most of them would probably warm to a friend.

有些人独来独往,喜欢离群索居,但无论多么独立,他们多数人对朋友也许很热情。

Those who are far from home, without family around them, know best the value of true friends.

远离家门并无家人陪伴的人最了解挚友的价值。

When a friendship begins, we notice everything that we have in common. When it ends, we realize how different we have been, all along.

友谊开始时,会注意与朋友之间所有的共同之处;友谊结束时,会意识到与对方一直就不是同类人。

With friends, whatever the differences in our experience of life, we feel a sense that we have all come from the same place.

与朋友在一起，不管生活经历如何，我们会感到都是来自同一地方。

It takes time and patience to build a friendship. In the beginning, don't be too needy. Wait until you know the person well before talking about your intimate problems.

建立友谊需要时间和耐心，不要一开始就急不可耐，熟悉后再谈自己的私密问题。

Cultivate the habit of gratitude. Write a gratitude diary, listing all the things that bring you joy in life, including your friends.

养成感恩的习惯，写感恩日记，列举所有带来快乐的事情，包括朋友。

A real friend is someone you imagine will still be there when you grow old.

真正的朋友是你老的时候你认为会依然与你相伴的人。

If you always have to be careful what you say to your friends, for fear they may pass on gossip, then they're not your true friends.

如果对朋友说话小心谨慎,怕被传出去,那么对方就不是真正的朋友。

The companions of our childhood always possess a certain power over our minds which hardly any later friend can obtain.

儿时玩伴在我们心中总有其位置,以后交的朋友几乎难以取代。

Plain food cooked by friends who love you may taste better than fancy food in a restaurant.

爱你的朋友做的粗茶淡饭比饭店的美食更好吃。

Be a friend to thyself, and others will be so too.

——Thomas Fuller

对自己友好,别人也会对你友好。

——托马斯·富勒

All friends get a little jealous of each other sometimes. However, beware the friends who are too jealous, for they are blinded by envy and truly cannot love you.

所有朋友都会有点相互嫉妒,但小心那些嫉妒心太重的人,被嫉妒蒙蔽的人不会真爱你。

True friends don't try to change us, unless we want to change ourselves.

真正的朋友不会努力改变我们,除非我们想改变自己。

The shifts of fortune test the reliability of friends.

命运的改变考验朋友是否可靠。

Friendships don't necessarily make you happy. But they should provide great comfort and companionship when you're feeling sad.

朋友不一定让你幸福,但在你难过时应该陪伴你,给你很大安慰。

After a sad event such as a bereavement or failure, a true friend can make life worth living once again.

遭受丧亲之痛或失败等厄运之后,真正的朋友会让你重新振作起来。

True friendship resists time, distance, and silence.

——Isabel Allende

真正的友谊历久弥新,天涯咫尺,不怕冷场。

——伊莎贝尔·阿兰德

With a good friend, you smile a little more often; anger a little less quickly. The sun shines a little brighter; and life is a little sweeter.

有个好朋友,你会微笑更多一些,气来得更慢一些,太阳更亮一些,生活更甜蜜一些。

Friendship is part of a long, happy marriage in which both partners like, as well as love, one another.

对相爱相悦的夫妻来说,友谊是长久幸福婚姻的组成部分。

In many cases, friendships are formed through shared interests or through working together, and may overcome big differences of personality and social background.

很多情况下,友谊源于共同爱好,一起工作,可以克服性格和社会背景的巨大差异。

Your best friend will tell you what you don't want to know.

最好的朋友会把你不爱听的事情告诉你。

It is not a lack of love, but a lack of friendship that makes unhappy marriages.

—— Friedrich Nietzsche

不幸福的婚姻不是缺乏爱情，而是缺乏友情。

——弗里德里希·尼采

A friendly, open, positive attitude to those you meet along life's way will always stand you in good stead. In most cases, you will find it an effective antidote to hostility, rudeness, and bad manners.

用友好开放的积极态度对待生命旅程中所遇到的人，总会让你处于有利的位置。在多数情况下你会发现这是对付敌意、粗鲁和无礼的有效方法。

Don't aim for success if you want it; just do what you love and believe in, and it will come naturally.

要成功，就不要追求成功；只要献身于热爱并信奉的事业，成功便会自然而至。

Love and be loved.

爱人者，人爱之。

Promises may get thee friends, but nonperformance will turn them into enemies.

许诺会为你赢得朋友，但食言则会化友为敌。

A true friend is the best possession.

真诚的朋友是最宝贵的财富。

The same man cannot be both friend and flatterer.

一个人不可能既是朋友,又是奉承者。

Ill company is like a dog who dirties those most that he loves best.

坏朋友就像狗一样,把人最喜爱的东西弄得肮脏不堪。

An open foe may prove a curse; but a pretended friend is worse.

公开的敌人是祸害,虚假的朋友则更坏。

Friends are made, not born.

朋友是结交的,并非天生的。

Friendship is a rose without a thorn.

友谊是不带刺的玫瑰。

Never trust friends who are indiscreet with your secrets.

Even if they do not mean to be malicious, they won't be able to stop themselves gossiping about your intimate revelations.

不要相信泄密的朋友，即使他们没有恶意，但却忍不住谈论你们的私交。

A new friend is always a mystery. He or she may turn out to be a friend for life, or just passing your way.

新朋友总是捉摸不透，也许会成为终生的朋友，也许只是生命中的过客。

There is magic in the memory of schoolboy friendships.

——Benjamin Disraeli

同学友谊的回忆具有神奇的魔力。

——本杰明·迪斯雷利

A cheerful friend is like the dawning of a sunny day: a joy to everyone.

快乐的朋友如同晴天的黎明，给每个人带来快乐。

Most friends have a great deal in common; but that doesn't go for all friends. Sometimes, close friends can be like chalk and cheese.

大多数朋友有很多共同点。但也并非都是如此，有时亲密的朋友之间毫无共同之处。

Close friends are like singers in harmony; you can't tell one voice from the other.

密友像和谐的合唱，分不清是谁的声音。

A firm friend will help you through times that are good, and times that are bad; times that are happy, and times that are sad.

挚友会与你同甘共苦，休戚与共。

Make time for your friends. They are the people who share your life, and help you to savour it.

抽时间与朋友相聚。朋友是与你共享生活，帮你体味生活的人。

It's good to have old friends, but always be prepared to make new ones.

拥有老朋友很好，但要随时准备结交新朋友。

Friendship is an essential part of a rich, full life; but solitude has its place, too.

友谊是丰富多彩生活的重要部分,独处也同样必不可少。

A friend is the person who is there for you when he'd rather be somewhere else.

本想去其他地方却为你而来的人便是朋友。

Regard everyone as a friend until they prove otherwise.

把每个人都视为朋友,结果发现都不是朋友。

Friendships are fragile, and need to be handled with care, just like any other valuable object.

友谊经不起折腾,要像对待宝贝一样小心保护。

Each person you meet may be a doorway to a new world.

你遇到的每个人都有可能让你进入一个全新世界。

Friendship nourishes the spirit.

友谊有益于精神健康。

Life is partly what you make it, and partly what it is made by the friends we choose.

生活一半是我们自己营造的,一半是我们选择的朋友营造的。

A smile costs nothing, but it has great value.

微笑不花钱,却价值不菲。

Friends are lost by calling too often, and calling too seldom.

经常拜访或很少拜访都会失去朋友。

Friendship is like money, easier made than kept.

友谊如钱,得来容易,留住难。

To be rich in friends is to be poor in nothing.

——Lilian Whiting

拥有很多朋友,必须样样不缺。

——莉莉安·怀廷

It is more shameful to distrust one's friends than to be deceived by them.

不信任朋友比被朋友欺骗更丢人。

Walking with a friend in the dark is better than walking alone in the light.

——Helen Keller

与朋友在黑暗中行走比独自在明亮中行走更好。

——海伦·凯勒

True friendship is a plant of slow growth and must undergo and withstand the shocks of adversity before it is entitled to the appellation.

——George Washington

真正的友谊须长时间培育,必须经历风风雨雨才会名副其实。

——乔治·华盛顿

Lose your temper and you lose a friend; lie, and you lose yourself.

发脾气失去朋友,撒谎失去自我。

Most of us have a best friend at each stage of life. The luckiest of us have the same one.

我们大多数在人生每个阶段都有最好的朋友,最幸运的是每个阶段的朋友是同一个人。

Many people walk in and out of your life, but a true friend leaves footprints on your heart.

——Eleanor Roosevelt

很多人进入或者离开你的生活，但是真正的朋友在你心里留下痕迹。

——埃莉诺·罗斯福

We are all travellers in the wilderness of this world, and the best we can find in our travels is an honest friend.

——Robert Louis Stevenson

我们都是这个世界荒原的游客，旅行中最好的发现就是真诚的朋友。

——罗伯特·路易斯·史蒂文森

Gratitude preserves old friendships, and procures new.

感恩留住老朋友，赢得新朋友。

Friendship with oneself is all-important, because without it, one cannot be friends with anybody else in the world.

——Eleanor Roosevelt

和自己交朋友很重要，否则不可能与任何人交朋友。

——埃莉诺·罗斯福

Let us learn to show our friendship for a man when he is alive, not after he is dead.

——F. Scott Fitzgerald

让我们对活着的人表示友好,而非在他死后。

——F·司各特·菲茨杰拉德

Friendship is the hardest thing in the world to explain. It's not something you learn in school.

友谊是世上最难讲清楚的事情,不是在学校学的东西。

A friend is a gift you give yourself.

——Robert Louis Stevenson

朋友是你给自己的礼物。

——罗伯特·路易斯·史蒂文森

It is one of the severest tests of friendship to tell your friend his faults. So to love a man that you cannot bear to see a stain upon him, and to speak painful truth through loving words, that is friendship.

——Henry Ward Beecher

把朋友的错误告诉他是严峻的考验。爱一个人不忍心看着他有污点,用爱的语言告知其痛苦事实,这便是友谊。

——亨利·沃德·比彻

Love delights in passion; friendship in tranquillity.

爱情喜欢激情,友谊喜欢平静。

A single rose can be my garden. A single friend, my world.

——Leo Buscaglia

一朵玫瑰可以是我的花园,一个朋友可以是我的世界。

——利奥·巴斯卡利亚

A true friend never holds you back, unless you are about to do something foolish.

真正的朋友从不会阻止你做事情,除非你要做蠢事。

Lots of people want to ride with you in the limo, but what you want is someone who will take the bus with you when the limo breaks down.

——Oprah Winfrey

很多人想搭乘你的小车。但是你想要的却是小车坏了的时候，与你一起乘公共汽车的人。

——奥普拉·温弗瑞

True happiness consists not in the multitude of friends, but in their worth and choice.

——Samuel Johnson

真正的幸福不在于有很多朋友，而是在于朋友的价值和选择。

——塞缪尔·约翰逊

Solitude and friendship are but two aspects of a healthy, well-balanced emotional life.

独处与友谊是有益于情感平衡的两个方面。

In friendship, as in marriage, opposites often attract.

友谊如同婚姻，完全不同的人之间会相互吸引。

In the language of flowers, a gift of red roses speaks of romantic love; pink roses, of affection; and yellow roses, of friendship and devotion.

不同颜色的花寓意不同。送红色玫瑰代表浪漫爱情，粉色玫瑰代表喜爱，黄色玫瑰代表友谊和忠诚。

A large age gap, or other significant difference, is no bar to friendship, for friendship knows no boundaries.

年龄或其他大的差异不妨碍友谊，友谊是没有界限的。

You are never alone when in the company of a good book.

有好书陪伴，绝不会孤独。

However much they age, our true friends always look beautiful to us — just as we hope to look beautiful to them.

无论年龄多大，真正的朋友总是看起来很漂亮，就像我们希望自己在他们眼里也很漂亮。

The two great companions of a lifetime are friendship and learning.

人生两个重要的陪伴就是友谊和学习。

You cannot be successful without making enemies, as well as friends.

不交朋友也不树敌你难以成功。

We learn much from our own mistakes; and more from our friends' mistakes.

我们从错误中吸取教训,从朋友的错误中吸取的教训更多。

Only your friends will tell you when your face is dirty.

——Spanish proverb

脸脏了,只有朋友会告诉你。

——西班牙谚语

Never injure a friend, even in jest.

——Cicero

即使是开玩笑也不要伤害朋友的感情。

——西塞罗

Give and take makes good friends.

有来有往,关系密切。

One who looks for a friend without faults will have none.

寻找完美朋友的人没有朋友。

A true friend wants nothing more from you than the pleasure of your company.

真正的朋友想得到与你相伴的快乐,别无他求。

He who walks with the wise grows wise, but a companion of fools suffers harm.

与智者相伴变得聪明,与愚者相伴遭受伤害。

The wise man remembers his friend at all times; the fool, only when he has need of them.

智者把朋友老是记挂在心,愚者只是遇到问题才想起朋友。

There is nothing on this earth more to be prized than true friendship.

——Thomas Aquinas

世上没有比友谊更珍贵的了。

——托马斯·阿奎奈

Friends and wine should be old.

朋友似酒,历久弥香。

The friendship that can cease has never been real.

——Saint Jerome

可以中断的友谊,绝非真正的友谊。

——圣杰罗姆

A quarrel between friends, when made up, adds a new tie to friendship.

朋友吵架和好后,友谊更加牢固。

Kindness gives birth to kindness.

——Sophocles

善善相生。

——索福克勒斯

Better to weep with wise men than to laugh with fools.

宁与智者哭,也不与愚者笑。

Good friends are the most important ingredient in the recipe for a long and happy life.

幸福长寿最重要的秘诀就是好友相伴。

Misfortune shows those who are not true friends.

——Aristotle

不幸暴露假朋友。

——亚里士多德

Money may make you wealthy, but a true friend makes you rich.

金钱让你富裕，挚友让你富足。

Friendship redoubleth joys, and cutteth grief in half.

——Francis Bacon

友谊使快乐加倍，使悲伤减半。

——弗朗西斯·培根

If we should forgive our enemies, how much more important it is that we should forgive our friends.

如果应该宽恕敌人，宽恕朋友更重要。

A person standing alone can be attacked and defeated, but two can stand back-to-back and conquer.

单枪匹马会遭受攻击和失败，两个人则可以相互保护战胜敌人。

A friend to all is a friend to none.

——Aristotle

所有人的朋友，谁的朋友也不是。

——亚里士多德

One who knows how to show and accept kindness will be a better friend than any.

——Sophocles

知道如何表示和接受善意是最好的朋友。

——索福克勒斯

The great success of your life is to have one or two really good friends.

人生重要的成功就是有一两个真正的朋友。

You are only complete when you have a true friend, someone who will share your joys and sorrows throughout life, and stand by you until the last.

有个真正的朋友，才算完美。这个人终生与你休戚与共，鼎力相助。

Social friends expect you to entertain them; real friends put up with you even when you're a bore.

社会朋友指望你给他们带来快乐，真正的朋友即使你讨厌，还是忍受你。

If you can't tell a friend the truth, the best option is to remain silent. Telling lies tends to lead to trouble, because lies are usually found out in the end.

如果不能告诉朋友事实,就保持沉默。撒谎会引起麻烦,因为谎言最终会被揭穿。

Don't ask too much of your friends— except occasionally, in emergencies.

除了危机之时偶尔求助外,不要老是麻烦朋友。

A good friend will help you in times of trouble. But if your life is a constant drama, he or she may tire of doing so.

好友会在你困难之时出手相助,但如果你麻烦不断,他们可能不愿意帮下去。

Making childish jokes is something we can only do in the company of our dearest friends.

只有在最亲密的朋友面前才可以开幼稚的玩笑。

Love for a friend can be deeper, and last longer, than romantic love.

友情可以比浪漫爱情更深厚持久。

Don't spend time with people who belittle your ambitions. You need friends who believe in you, so that you can start to believe in yourself.

不要与轻视你的志向的人交往,你需要信任你的朋友来逐步建立自信。

No better relation than a prudent and faithful friend.

最好的关系莫过于谨慎忠诚的朋友。

Give your friend the most precious gift you have to offer. Your time.

给朋友你所拥有的最好礼物——时间。

Borrow money from a bank, rather than from your friends.

从银行借钱,不要向朋友借钱。

We can see the faults in our friends quite clearly; in ourselves, less so.

我们能看清楚朋友的毛病,对自己的毛病却看不太清楚。

The seven rules of friendship: Keep your appointments; Remember birthdays; Enquire after relatives; Don't borrow money, and if you do, pay it back quickly; Listen more than you speak; Don't criticize your friend's partner, children, or family; Be discreet。

友谊七规则：守约；记着生日；问候朋友家人；不借钱，借了快还；多听少说；不要批评朋友的配偶、孩子或家庭；谨慎行事。

When you meet new people, don't jump to conclusions. Sometimes, a person you take an immediate dislike to may turn out to become a firm friend.

不要对新结识的人急于下结论，有时开始不喜欢的人结果成了挚友。

No distance of place or lapse of time can lessen the friendship of those who are thoroughly persuaded of each other's worth.

——Robert Southey

距离和时间不能削弱相互珍重的朋友之间的友谊。

——罗伯特·骚塞

Only as we grow older do we really appreciate the gift of having true, loyal, and loving friends.

年纪大了,才会珍视爱你的忠实挚友。

The key of love opens the door of friendship.

爱的钥匙才能打开友谊之门。

A friend is the first person you want to call when you hear good news.

朋友是你听到好消息第一个想告知的人。

Fiends are more important than lovers. Lovers come and go, but a good friend will stick with you throughout your life.

朋友比情人更重要。情人来去不定,好朋友终生相伴。

If you have even one friend you can trust completely, and rely on absolutely, then you are the luckiest person in the world.

如果有哪怕一个完全信任、绝对依赖的朋友,你就是世界上最幸运的人。

If friends live far away, make an effort to keep in touch. A simple Christmas or birthday card, a phone call, or a letter, will help to keep your friendship strong.

如果朋友住在远方，要努力保持接触，一个简单的圣诞卡、生日卡、一个电话或一封信都有助于巩固友谊。

Friendship is like an olive tree: it shades us in summer; provides fruit for us in winter; shows us sweet flowers; and has leaves that are evergreen. It is firmly planted in the soil, and however strong the winds may blow, it cannot be uprooted.

友谊像橄榄树，夏天遮阴，冬天有果，鲜花养眼，绿叶长青，根深抗风。

No love, no friendship can cross the path of our destiny without leaving some mark on it forever.

——François Mauri

爱情与友谊都会在我们命运的途中留下一些永久的痕迹。

——弗朗索瓦·毛利

If fortune does not favour you, your faithful friends will have to do.

如果命运没有关照你,忠实的朋友只好关照你。

Treasure your friends, for they are the ones who bring light into your life.

珍视朋友,他们是给你的生活带来光明的人。

Trouble is a sieve through which we sift our acquaintances. Those too big to pass through are our friends.

——Arlene Francis

困境是个筛选熟人的筛子。没有从网眼里筛出去的熟人便是朋友。

——阿琳·弗朗西斯

To be capable of steady friendship or lasting love, are the two greatest proofs, not only of goodness of heart, but of strength of mind.

——William Hazlitt

能够保持稳固的友谊和持久的爱,最能证明善良与恒心。

——威廉·哈兹里特

Friendship is the selfless form of love.

友谊是一种无私的爱。

Parents and children can form friendships with each other; on the other hand, they may not be temperamentally suited to do so. If you find friendship in your family, enjoy it; if not, accept that they love you, and you love them, which should be enough.

父母与子女可以成为朋友,也可能脾气不相投,难以成为朋友。有友情,就享受家人的友情,脾气不相投,知道他们爱你,你爱他们就已足够。

A garden is a friend that you can visit whenever you feel like it.

庭院是你可以随时造访的朋友。

Good friends give advice; best friends listen.

好朋友提建议,最好的朋友只是洗耳恭听。

As time passes, we often become separated from our friends. They go to live in different cities, or countries, start families, make new friends. If you want to keep in touch, make sure you organize visits occasionally if possible – travel to where they live, have them to stay, or meet somewhere halfway between your homes.

随着时间推移，我们常常会与朋友分手。他们到另外的城市或农村生活或建立家庭，或结交新朋友。想保持联系可以偶尔见见面——登门拜访，留宿，或在两个家庭之间某个地方见面。

Friendship can be a demanding occupation. If you have a lot of friends, it may be that you're not giving as much as you should to each of them.

友谊需要应酬。朋友太多，就无法一一满足。

When befriended, remember it; when you befriend, forget it.

受人恩惠，铭记在心；施恩与人，不放心上。

Do not all you can, spend not all you have, believe not all you hear, and tell not all you know.

不要做尽所能，不要花尽所有，不要全信所闻，不要言尽所知。

A clear conscience is a sure card.

光明磊落，胜券在握。

There is a time to speak and a time to be silent.

——Caxton

该说话时说话,该沉默时沉默。

——卡克斯顿

Animals are such agreeable friends——they ask no questions, they pass no criticisms.

——George Eliot

动物是称心如意的朋友——从不提问,也从不批评。

——乔治·艾略特

Honest criticism is hard to take, particularly from a relative, a friend, an acquaintance, or a stranger.

——Eleanor Roosevelt

坦诚的批评难以接受,尤其那些来自亲戚、朋友、熟人或陌生人的批评更难接受。

——埃莉诺·罗斯福

It is impossible to defeat an ignorant man in argument.

——W. G. Mcadoo

在争论中是无法击败无知者的。

——W·G·麦卡杜

Mutual forgiveness of each vice, such are the gates of Paradise.

——William Blake

相互宽容乃是天堂之门。

——威廉·布莱克

We build too many walls and not enough bridges.

——Isaac Newton

人与人之间建起了太多的围墙,却没有建造足够多的桥梁。

——艾萨克·牛顿

He who in adversity would have succor, should be generous while he rests secure.

——Saki

谁想在逆境中得到援助,就应在身处顺境时待人宽厚。

——萨基

To make a lasting marriage we have to overcome self-centeredness.

——George Gordon Byron

要使婚姻持久，就要克服自我中心意识。

——乔治·戈登·拜伦

Follow your own course, and let people talk.

——A. Dante

走自己的路，让别人去说吧。

——A·但丁

The measure of a man's real character is what he would do if he knew he would never be found out.

——Thomas B. Macaulay

衡量一个人真正的品质，要看他在知道自己可能永远也不会受到重视的情况下做些什么。

——托马斯·B·麦考利

Treat other people as you hope they will treat you.

——Aesop

希望别人如何对待你，你就如何对待别人。

——伊索

A blind man will not thank you for a looking glass.

盲人不谢赠镜人。

A covetous man is good to none, but worst to himself.

贪婪者于他人无益,于己害处更大。

A crooked stick will have a crooked shadow.

身不正,影必斜。

A dog will not howl if you beat him with a bone.

肉骨头打狗,狗不叫。

A friend in word is never a friend of mine.

口头上的朋友绝不是朋友。

A friend is easier lost than found.

朋友易失不易得。

A good husband makes a good wife. A good Jack makes a good Jill.

丈夫好,妻子也好。两好合一好。

Those who bring sunshine into the lives of others cannot keep it from themselves.

给别人生活送去灿烂的阳光，自己的生活也就充满了阳光。

Man will occasionally stumble over the truth, but most of the time he will pick himself up and continue on.

——Winston Churchill

人有时会因说实话而栽跟斗，但是多数情况下他会振作精神，继续前进。

——温斯顿·丘吉尔

Be slow to promise and quick to perform.

不轻诺，诺必果。

A tree is known by its fruit.

观其行而知其人。

A true friend is known in the day of adversity.

疾风知劲草，患难见真情。

A man knows his companion in a long journey and a little inn.

路遥知马力，日久见人心。

A clear conscience laughs at false accusations.

不做亏心事，敲门心不惊。

Be just to all, but trust not all.

要公正对待所有的人，但不要轻信所有的人。

Believe not all that you see nor half what you hear.

眼见的不能全信，耳闻的不能半信。

Be swift to hear, slow to speak.

多听少说。

Manners maketh man.

——William Wykeham

礼节造就人。

——威廉·维克汉姆

Politeness and consideration for others is like investing pennies and getting dollars back.

——Thomas Sowell

以礼待人、体贴周到好比投资便士，收获美元。

——托马斯·索维尔

Wherever you go, no matter what the weather, always bring your own sunshine.

——Anthony J. D'Angelo

无论你走到哪里，无论什么天气，永远带上你的阳光。

——安瑟尼·J·德安格罗

You shouldn't say it is not good. You should say you do not like it; and then, you know, you're perfectly safe.

——James Whistler

不应该说那不好，而应该说你不喜欢那样。你知道这样你就绝对安全了。

——詹姆斯·威斯特勒

Handle them carefully, for words have more power than atom bombs.

——Pearl S. Hurd

说话要慎重，因为言辞的威力胜过原子弹。

——波尔·S·胡德

When you blame others, you give up your power to change.

——Douglas N. Adams

你抱怨他人时，就放弃了改变现状的权利。

——道格拉斯·N·亚当斯

The best thing to give to your enemy is forgiveness; to an opponent, tolerance; to a friend, your heart; to your child, a good example; to a father, deference; to your mother, conduct that will make her proud of you; to yourself, respect; to all men, charity.

宽恕敌人，容忍对手，诚心待友，为子师表，敬重父亲，为母增光，自尊自重，善待他人，是最好的处世之道。

Networking in professional, social, and other settings has become an increasingly important aspect of a job search as people now tend to move from one company to another more frequently.

——Leslie Tebbe

由于现在人们更加频繁地从一个公司转到另一个公司，所以无论在职场上、社会上还是在其他场合，人际网络已经成为求职的一部分，其重要性与日俱增。

——莱斯利·特彼

Networking—making potentially useful contacts and building relationships with individuals, groups, and organizations—has been, and remains, an integral factor in business.

——Jeff Davidson

人际网络——可以为将来建立有用的人际关系，与个人、群体和组织建立起联系——曾经是而且依然是职场生涯的组成部分。

——杰弗·戴维森

You can buy a person's hands but you can't buy his heart. His heart is where his enthusiasm, his loyalty is.

——Stephen Covey

你可以买到一个人的双手但却买不到他的心。他的心就是他的热情和忠诚之所在。

——史蒂芬·柯维

Be nice to people on your way up because you may meet them on your way down.

——Jimmy Durante

你在上坡的时候要待人和蔼可亲，因为你也许会在下坡的时候与他们再次相遇。

——杰米·达朗迪

Greeting cards are an effective tool for establishing new business relationships. Cards can pave the way for a smooth first meeting by making a favorable impression and relieving the awkwardness of initial contacts.

贺卡是建立新业务伙伴关系的有效工具。贺卡能给对方留下良好的印象,能让初次相见的双方摆脱尴尬,为初次见面的顺利进行铺垫了道路。

To have respect for ourselves guides our morals; and to have a deference for others governs our manners.

——Lawrence Sterne

尊重自己让我们品行高尚;尊重他人让我们举止得体。

——劳伦斯·斯特恩

Admonish your friends in private, praise them in public.

私下里要忠告你的朋友,在公开场合表扬朋友。

A faithful friend is hard to find.

挚友难得。

A man has two ears and one mouth that he may hear much and speak little.

人有两只耳朵一张嘴，就是为了多听少说。

Answer a fool according to his folly.
以其人之道，还治其人之身。

A silent tongue and true heart are the most admirable things on earth.
世上最令人羡慕的是一张缄默的嘴和一颗真诚的心。

A word spoken is an arrow let fly.
一言既出，驷马难追。

A friend to everybody is a friend to nobody.
广交友，无朋友。

A good fame is better than a good face.
好的名声胜于好的相貌。

A good name is sooner lost than won.
美誉难得而易失。

A great talker is a great liar.
最会饶舌的人也是最会说谎的人。

All are not merry that dance lightly.
轻盈起舞者，未必都快乐。

All are not saints that go to church.
去做礼拜者，未必皆圣人。

A man is not good or bad for one action.
不能凭一次行为判断人的好坏。

A middle course is the safest.
中庸之道最保险。

A true friend is one soul in two bodies.
真正的朋友肝胆相照。

Better an open enemy than a false friend.
公开的敌人胜于虚假的朋友。

Better the foot slip than the tongue trip.
宁可摔跤，不可失言。

Better to do well than to say well.
说得好不如做得好。

Do not cut down the tree that gives you shade.

不要砍倒为你遮阴的大树。

Do not give a dog bread every time he wags his tail.

不要有求必应。

Do not praise a day before sunset.

切勿褒贬过早。

Do not to others what you do not wish them to do to you.

己所不欲,勿施于人。

Eagles catch no flies.

鹰不捕蝇,大人物不计较小事情。

Envy assails the noblest, the winds howl around the highest peak.

高位遭人妒,高峰招风吹。

Fall sick and you will see who is your friend and who is not.

患难见真情。

Forgive others but not yourself.

严于律己，宽以待人。

Friendship cannot stand always on one side.

来而不往非礼也。

Good for good every man can do; good for bad only a noble man can do.

以德报德，人人都能做到；以德报怨只有高尚的人才能做到。

Govern your thoughts when alone, and your tongue when in company.

一人独处慎于思，与人相处慎于言。

He that is ill to himself will be good to nobody.

不知自爱的人也不会爱别人。

The sting of a reproach is the truth of it.

指责带给你的刺痛，正是它的真实之处。

One loses by pride and gains by modesty.

满招损，谦受益。

Never bow to authority, but always tip your hat.

应向有权者敬礼，不应向他屈膝。

He that would govern others first should be the master of himself.

要管好别人，先管好自己。

Don't value a man for the quality he is of, but for the quality he possesses.

地位不要紧，着重看人品。

Better the devil you know than the devil you don't know.

明枪易躲，暗箭难防。

Better the last smile than the first laughter.

宁可最后微笑，不要首先狂喜。

Better a frank denial than unwilling compliance.

勉强应允不如坦诚拒绝。

Be wisely worldly, be not worldly wise.

要聪明地世故，不要世故地聪明。

All for one, one for all.

人人为我，我为人人。

A fall into the pit, a gain in your wit.

吃一堑，长一智。

A penny soul never comes to two pennies.

心胸狭窄，一事无成。

Bargain has neither friends nor relations.

交易面前无亲友。

A willing helper does not wait until he is asked.

愿助人者总是主动帮助别人。

Do as most men do and men will speak well of thee.

照大多数人那样干，人们会把你称赞。

If you ride a horse, sit close and tight; if you ride a man, sit easy and light.

骑马应紧贴马背，待人则应平和可亲。

If you would be loved, love and be loveable.

若欲被人爱,需爱人且可爱。

Grasp all, lose all.

贪者必失。

Honesty is the best policy.

诚实为上策。

Men are not to be measured in inches.

海水不可斗量,人不可貌相。

The most exhausting thing in life is being insincere.

——A. M. Lindbergh

生活中最使人筋疲力尽的事是弄虚作假。

——A·M·林德伯格

I've never had any pity for conceited people, because I think they carry their comfort about with them.

——George Eliot

我从不怜悯自负的人,我觉得他们总是自鸣得意。

——乔治·艾略特

Bring up a raven and he'll pick out your eyes.

养虎遗患。

A man may dig his grave with his teeth.

祸从口出。

A man may lead a horse to the water, but he cannot make him drink.

牵马到河易,逼马饮水难。

A quarrelsome man has no good neighbors.

好争吵者无好邻居。

Listening is a skill. Unfortunately, we are far better talkers than we are listeners. But you can't be a good speaker without being a good listener. One skill relies on the other.

聆听是一门技巧。遗憾的是,我们更善谈而不善听。然而不善听就难以善谈。这两项技巧相辅相成,相互依存。

To do injustice is more disgraceful than to suffer it.

——Plato

待人不公比遭遇不公更可耻。

——柏拉图

In a way, nobody sees a flower really. It is so small; we haven't time. And to see takes time, as to have a friend takes time.

——Georgia O'Keeffe

在某种意义上，没有人真正观赏过一朵花。花那么小，我们又没有时间。赏花是要花时间的，就像交朋友一样。

——乔治亚·奥基夫

Great men are rarely isolated mountain peaks; they are summits of ranges.

——T. W. Higginson

伟人很少是突兀的山峰；他们是众山中的最高峰。

——T·W·希金森

Plant your feet, look at them in the eye, and tell the truth.

站稳脚跟，正视对方，实话实说。

The one who has an excessively remarkable character is often hard to shelter oneself in the society.

性格过分突出的人往往难以容身于社会。

Flowers are prettiest in half bloom. Wines are at their best when we are half drunk.

花看半开,酒饮微醉。

The art of conversation lies not in what you ought to say, but in what one ought not to say.

谈话的艺术不在于该说什么,而在于不该说什么。

Learn to say no. It will be of more use than to be able to read Latin.

要学会说不。这要比会读拉丁文更管用。

Silence is a great art of conversation.

沉默是一门重要的对话艺术。

Dress like a bum and you act like a bum. Dress like a gentleman and you act like a gentleman.

穿得像流浪汉,你的行为就像流浪汉。穿得像绅士,你的行为就像绅士。

Kindnesses are easily forgotten; but injuries are often remembered.

忘却受到的恩惠易,忘掉受到的伤害难。

Don't readily believe in any scandals, except you have the exact evidence.

除非证据确凿,别轻信流言蜚语。

If a person refuses to hear others' advice, this will do him no good; but if he follows whatever advice people might offer him, this will do him even greater harm.

拒纳他人言,于己无益;广纳他人言,于己更无益。

Let us never negotiate out of fear, but let us never fear to negotiate.

我们决不要因害怕而去谈判,但也决不能害怕谈判。

Curiosity is ill manners in another's house.

在别人家里显得好奇,是没有修养的表现。

It is more tolerable to be refused than deceived.

被拒绝总比被欺骗好。

Tell your secret to your servant, and he'll become your master.

把隐私告诉仆人,他会成为你的主人。

Flattery is a wine that suits everybody's taste.

奉承是适合所有人口味的一种酒。

You cannot burn the candle at both ends.

蜡烛不能两头都烧。

Guard against those who fawn upon you and bow obsequiously before you.

谁要是对你阿谀奉承,点头哈腰,可要保持警惕。

Silence is one of the hardest arguments to refute.

沉默是最难反驳的争论方式之一。

The deepest feeling always shows itself in silence.

最深的感情总是以沉默方式出现。

Never be haughty to the humble; never be humble to the haughty.

不要对谦恭自卑者趾高气扬，也不要对趾高气扬者谦恭自卑。

The better you treat little minds, the better you are protected.

待小人越宽，自己越安全。

Arrogance is a kind of unsupported dignity.

傲慢是一种得不到支持的尊严。

Silence is the sovereign contempt.

沉默是最大的鄙视。

When the enemy praises you, you should ask yourself what errors you have committed.

当敌人赞扬你时，你应该扪心自问你做错了什么。

Yearn to understand first and to be understood second.

盼望被别人理解，首先要理解别人。

Don't do anything that takes away from your self-respect.

别做有悖自尊的任何傻事。

Frugality is a handsome income.

节俭是一笔可观的收入。

One must be modest at childhood, steady at youth, just at middle age, careful at old age.

童年时要谦逊,青年时要稳健,成年时要公正,暮年时要谨慎。

He that cannot forgive others breaks the bridge over which he must pass himself, for every man has need to be forgiven.

不能原谅别人等于毁掉了必须经过的桥,因为每个人都有需要别人原谅的时候。

Borrowing dulls the edge of husbandry.

靠借贷度日就会忘掉节俭。

Love your neighbor —yet don't pull down your hedge.

爱你的邻居,但不要拆掉篱笆。

Well-timed silence has more eloquence than speech.

适时沉默胜于雄辩。

Arrogance is the termite of interpersonal relations.

傲慢是人际关系中的破坏者。

It takes strength to hide your own pains; it takes courage to show them.

隐藏自己的痛苦需要力量；展示自己的痛苦需要勇气。

An intemperate advocate is more dangerous than an open foe.

狂热的吹捧者比公开的敌人更危险。

Don't cut the bough you are standing on.

别把脚下的树枝砍断。

A man can't ride your back unless it's bent.

你的腰不弯,别人就不能骑到你背上。

Revenge is dangerous; it hurts both your enemy and yourself.

报复是危险的,它使人两败俱伤。

A man never discloses his own character so clearly as when he describes another's.

一个人在描述别人的性格时最能暴露出自己的性格。

Better to be occasionally cheated than perpetually suspicious.

偶尔受骗比总是怀疑好。

There are no menial jobs, only menial attitudes.

没有低贱的工作,只有低贱的态度。

Flying into a rage on the slightest provocation is the evidence of indulgence and lack of education.

动辄发怒是放纵和缺乏教养的表现。

Censuring others for lacking education shows that, this person is also in short of education.

指责旁人没有教养的人,表明其本身同样缺乏教养。

Cooperation is doing with a smile what you have to do anyhow.

合作就是面带笑容去做非做不可的事。

A man belittles himself and others will belittle him.

一个人小看自己,别人也会小看他。

Interpersonal relations are a kind of social capital. If you keep them long, you must economize them.

人际关系是一种社会资本,想长久拥有就得节约使用。

If individuality has no play, the society won't advance; if individuality breaks out of all bounds, the society will perish.

个性不张扬,社会无进步; 个性毁约束,社会将崩溃。

Working together works.

—— Rob Gilbert

众人拾柴火焰高。

——罗伯·吉尔伯特

Problems can become opportunities when the right people come together.

——Robert Redford

合适的人凑在一起会把困难变机会。

——罗伯特·雷德福

You can work miracles by having faith in others. To get the best out of people, choose to think and believe the best about them.

——Bob Moawad

信任会产生奇迹,要让大家充分发挥作用,就要相信他们是最优秀的人。

——鲍勃·莫瓦德

If you're too busy to help those around you succeed, you're too busy.

——Bob Moawad

如果忙得顾不得身边的人获得成功,那就是忙过了头。

——鲍勃·莫瓦德

The best minute you spend is the one you invest in people.

赢得好人缘,回报最丰厚。

If he works for you, you work for him.

他为你工作,你就为他工作。

Nobody can avoid coming into conflicts with others. He has to push through the crowd in different ways, offending others while being offended.

在生活中，谁也无法避免与别人发生冲突，不得不以各种方式奋力挤过人群，在冒犯别人的同时也忍受别人的冒犯。

The deepest principle of human nature is the craving to be appreciated.

——William James

渴望被赞美是人性最深处的渴求。

——威廉·詹姆斯

Life is a blanket that is too short. Wrap it up and your toes will show; pull it down and your shoulders will catch cold. The optimist, however, can spend a good night curling up their knees.

人生是一块太短的毯子。裹上它，脚趾会露出来；拉下去，肩膀又冷。乐观者可以屈膝度良宵。

When you plan to get even with someone, you are only letting that person continue to hurt you.

打算报复,只是在让那个人继续伤害你。

A soft answer turns away wrath.
软话足以息怒。

What can't be cured must be endured.
不能解决的问题只得忍耐。

He has no friend who has many friends.

——Aristotle

广交友者无知己。

——亚里士多德

When you're good to others, you are best to yourself.
善待他人,即善待自己。

He that respects not is not respected.
不尊重他人者,亦得不到别人的尊重。

Let every man be respected as an individual and no man idolized.

——A. Einstein

让每个人作为个人受到尊重,但不要让任何人成为偶像。

——A·爱因斯坦

To really understand a man we must judge him in misfortune.

——Napoleon Bonaparte

要真正了解一个人,需在危难中考察他。

——拿破仑·波拿巴

One always speaks badly when he has nothing to speak.

一个人无话可说的时候,说话效果总是最差的。

Many of us are shy, but if we ask the right questions, small talk can serve us as a way to build meaningful relationships.

——Fine

多数人都很害羞,但是如果我们提问得体,聊天就有助于建立起有意义的人际关系。

——范妮

I don't like that man. I must get to know him better.

——Abraham Lincoln

我不喜欢那个人。我必须更好地去了解他。

——亚伯拉罕·林肯

If you board the wrong train, it is no use running along the corridor in the other direction.

上错火车,在车厢里向相反的方向跑也无济于事。

Do not pursue what is illusory — property and position: all that is gained at the expense of your nerves decade after decade and can be confiscated in one fell night.

—— Alexander Solzhenitsyn

不要追求虚幻的东西——财富与地位。年复一年,殚精竭虑获取的财富与地位,会在厄运降临时,一夜之间化为乌有。

——亚历山大·索尔仁尼琴

Nothing can bring you peace, but yourself.

——Ralph Waldo Emerson

除了自己谁也不能让自己心灵平静。

——拉尔夫·瓦尔多·爱默生

Originality and a feeling of one's own dignity are achieved only through work and struggle.

创造性与尊严感只有通过工作与奋斗才能获得。

Take your time to make an important decision, but once you have made it, don't look back.

不要急于做重要决定，一旦决定，义无反顾。

Conversation with a wise person can be more enlightening than years of reading books.

与智者一席话，胜读多年书。

Feeling gratitude and not expressing it is like wrapping a present and not giving it.

——William Arthur Ward

心存感激，不愿说出口，如同把礼物包起来不送出去。

——威廉·阿瑟·沃德

One should examine oneself for a very long time before thinking of condemning others.

谴责别人之前要先长时间审视自己。

The best form of protection is to keep out of harm's way.

最好的保护就是远离伤害。

Ask for advice from those with a wide experience of life, not those with a wide experience of books.

要向生活经验丰富和博学的人请教,而不要向书呆子请教。

Danger and delight often dwell together.

乐极生悲。

Every form of addiction is bad, no matter whether the narcotic be alcohol or morphine or idealism.

——Carl Jung

任何形式的上瘾都是不好的,不管上瘾的是酒精、吗啡,还是理想主义。

——卡尔·荣格

A servant is known by his master's absence.

主人不在场可以看出仆人的品行。

Men are like wine: some turn to vinegar, but the best improve with age.

人就像葡萄酒:有的会变酸,而最好的历久弥香。

We are all alike, on the inside.

——Mark Twain

在内心我们都很相像。

——马克·吐温

Speak well of your friends; say nothing of your enemies.

赞扬朋友，不谈敌人。

Life is the first gift, love the second, and understanding the third.

——Marge Piercv

生命是第一个礼物，爱是第二个礼物，理解是第三个礼物。

——玛吉·皮尔克夫

Be not angry that you cannot make others as you wish them to be, since you cannot make yourself as you wish yourself to be.

——Thomas Kempis

不要因为别人没有达到你的期望值而恼火，因为你自己也不能达到自己的期望值。

——托马斯·肯比斯

You don't have to have an opinion on everything.

无须事事发表意见。

We judge ourselves by what we feel capable of doing, while others judge us by what we have already done.

—— Henry Wadsworth Longfellow

自我判断根据自己感觉所能胜任的事，他人判断我们根据我们的所作所为。

——亨利·沃兹沃斯·朗费罗

A man apt to promise is apt to forget.

轻诺者易忘。

It is the nature of a fool to see the faults of others and forget his own.

——Cicero

只看见别人的错误而忘记自己缺点是蠢人的本性。

——西塞罗

As you grow older, try to avoid living in the past.

随着年龄增长，要避免怀旧。

Do not listen to what people say; look at what they do.

不要听其言，而要观其行。

Honesty is all you need.

——Cass Elliot

诚实是立身之本。

——卡斯·艾略特

Patience! The windmill never strays in search of the wind.

——Andy J. Sklivis

耐心等待！风车从不跑去找风。

——安迪·J·斯克利维斯

You can dream, create, design, and build the most wonderful idea in the world, but it requires people to make the dream a reality.

——Walt Disney

你可以梦想，创作，设计，让创意登峰造极，但是梦想的实现要靠大家。

——沃特·迪斯尼